The Hubble Space
Telescope

The Hubble Space Telescope

Ray Spangenburg and Kit Moser

Franklin Watts

A DIVISION OF SCHOLASTIC INC.
NEW YORK · TORONTO · LONDON · AUCKLAND · SYDNEY
MEXICO CITY · NEW DELHI · HONG KONG
DANBURY, CONNECTICUT

To
SKYWATCHERS EVERYWHERE,
both amateur and professional.

Photographs © 2002: Ancient Art & Architecture Collection Ltd.: 15; Barbara Gentile: 80; Corbis-Bettmann: 36, 39, 75, 109; Hulton|Archive/Getty Images: 30 (Earl Young), 16, 65, 117; NASA: 82, 83 (John Bahcall/Institute for Advanced Study, Princeton), 8 (Matt Bobrowsky/OSC), 45, 54, 55 (Goddard Space Flight Center), 84 (Jeff Hester and Paul Scowen/Arizona State University), 88, 118 (Jon Morse, University of Colorado), 32 (NOAO/ESA/The Hubble Heritage Team), 2, 10, 17, 18, 25, 38, 41, 42, 48, 52, 68, 71, 79, 90, 94, 100, 110, 113, 114, 121, 122 127; North Wind Picture Archives: 22; Photo Researchers, NY: 21 (Dr. Jeremy Burgess/SPL), 24 (Simon Fraser/SPL), 60, 96, 97 (NASA/SPL), 58 (NASA/SS), 12 (Jerry Schad), 92 (STSI/NASA/SPL); Photri-Microstock: cover.

The photograph on the cover shows an artist's rendition of the *Hubble Space Telescope* launch. The photograph opposite the title page shows the *Hubble Space Telescope* in the space shuttle *Endeavour*'s cargo bay.

Library of Congress Cataloging-in-Publication Data

Spangenburg, Ray, 1939-
    The Hubble space telescope / Ray Spangenburg and Kit Moser.
        p. cm.—(Out of this world)
    Includes bibliographical references and index.
    ISBN 0-531-11894-0 (lib. bdg)   0-531-15565-X   (pbk.)
    1. Hubble Space Telescope—Juvenile literature. [Hubble Space Telescope
(Spacecraft) 2. Telescopes. 3. Outer space—Exploration.] I.Moser, Diane, 1944-
II. Title.   III. Out of this world (Franklin Watts, Inc.)

QB500.268 .S65 2002
522'.2919—dc21   2001017563

Acknowledgments

To all those who have contributed to *The Hubble Space Telescope,* we would like to take this opportunity to say thank you. A word of appreciation goes to our editors, Melissa Palestro and Melissa Stewart, whose steady flow of creativity, energy, enthusiasm, and dedication has infused this series. We would also like to thank Sam Storch, lecturer at the American Museum-Hayden Planetarium, and Margaret Carruthers, M.S. in planetary geology, Oxford, England, who both reviewed the manuscript and made many insightful suggestions. Also, to Tony Reichhardt and John Rhea, our editors at the former *Space World Magazine*, thanks for starting us out on many fascinating journeys into space, space science, and technology—including a visit to see the *Hubble Space Telescope* when it was still in a Lockheed clean room on the West Coast.

Contents

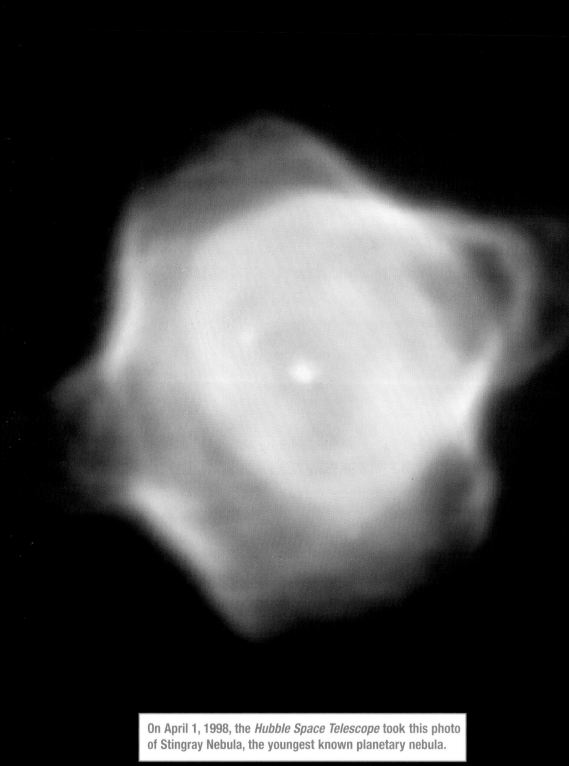

On April 1, 1998, the *Hubble Space Telescope* took this photo of Stingray Nebula, the youngest known planetary nebula.

Spectacular Visions

About the size of a school bus, orbiting 381 miles (613 kilometers) above Earth, the *Hubble Space Telescope* looks out into the darkness of space. Alone, without a crew, it is an electronic servant to humankind. Its job: to find sources of light and examine them closely. From Earth, without a telescope, these lights seem tiny in the nighttime skies. From *Hubble*'s position in orbit, though, these lights are spectacular visions, never before seen by anyone.

Hubble's eye is ever-observant. Look, there is a supernova. Look, there, millions of miles away, galaxies collide. Look again and see *quasars* blinking and evidence of matter falling into massive black holes.

Report to Earth, to the questing humans far below. Report the magnificent sights, the mysteries of time and of space. Report the clusters of

Following *Hubble*'s successful maintenance and update visit to the space shuttle *Discovery*'s pay-load bay in December 1999, astronauts took this image of the *Hubble Space Telescope*.

stars being born and the signs of dying stars in the last stages of life. Report on the red giants—brilliant, massive, and cool. Report on the white dwarfs, beaming for the last of their days. Report quietly, in the blink of an eye. Report and report again, turned toward the astonishing mysteries of the great night circus of the universe.

Far below, covered by a great shroud of atmosphere, the astronomers and the scientists watch, see, and learn from the great eye. Like a gigantic electronic periscope above the city lights, above the shimmering distortion caused by Earth's atmosphere and the ceiling of swirling storm clouds, *Hubble* gazes out into the darkness of space.

The Milky Way as seen from Mount Rainier National Park in Washington State.

Chapter 1

A New Kind of Vision

People have been looking up at the nighttime skies since prehistoric times. The tiny lights they saw winking and glittering there set them to thinking and wondering. These objects were mysterious, and people of different cultures had many ideas about what they could be.

Perhaps the sky was a giant, black, upside-down bowl with holes in it and the light they saw came from outside and was shining through the holes. Perhaps the heavens were perfect spheres of crystal, one within another, and the stars were hung on the outermost sphere. Each culture devised its own explanation. Some early cultures made careful studies of the movements of the stars, Sun, Moon, and planets. For example, Babylonian astronomers gathered facts they observed about the stars more than four thousand years ago and recorded them on stone tablets. Then they created calendars based on their records. Using these, they could help predict floods and the right time to plant crops.

Early astronomers soon began to develop tools for measuring distances between stars and other objects and for calculating their movements. However, not until the invention of the telescope could anyone really see much of what was happening in the vast universe around us. Stars appeared to be faint pinpoints of light shining through a dark canopy. The planets seemed to be "wandering stars." They looked similar to stars, yet their orbits made them seem to wander around in the sky against the steadier background of stars. No one had ever seen the surface of a planet or a close-up photo of the Moon's surface. The invention of the *telescope* in the seventeenth century began to change all that. Only then did astronomers begin to see that these objects were all worlds in their own right.

Galileo's Magnifying Tube

Telescopes are not ancient. They are "only" about four hundred years old. The word comes originally from a Greek word, *teleskopos,* which itself came from the words *tele* (meaning "far-seeing") and *skopos* (meaning "watcher"). The idea of using lenses in a tube to see faraway objects may have originated with early spectacle makers in Italy. The English philosopher and teacher Roger Bacon (c.1220–92)—famous for his promotion of experimental science—also may have played with the concept in the thirteenth century. According to stories of the time, though, the manufacture of the first telescope was an accident. In about 1608 a Dutch optician named Hans Lippershey (c.1570–c.1619) happened to line up two lenses that had just the right qualities. In his hands was an instrument that made faraway objects appear much closer.

Soon people began using telescopes for spotting faraway ships as they appeared along the horizon, filled with goods for trade and traveling loved ones. The great Italian astronomer Galileo Galilei (1564–1642) heard about Lippershey's trick with lenses within a few months. He began building his own optic tubes that were patterned after Lippershey's original.

Galileo used a long tube that contained two lenses, which allowed him to see objects ten times farther away than anyone else ever had. Then Galileo had a bright idea. Why not use his telescope to look at the nighttime skies? Beginning in 1609 he turned his telescope to the skies night after night.

Galileo's telescope was primitive by today's standards. A telescope you can buy in a toy store has better lenses with fewer flaws

These two telescopes belonged to Galileo and are on display at the Tribuna di Galileo in Florence, Italy. The glass mounted in the center of the ivory frame is a piece of the broken object glass Galileo used when he discovered the four satellites of Jupiter.

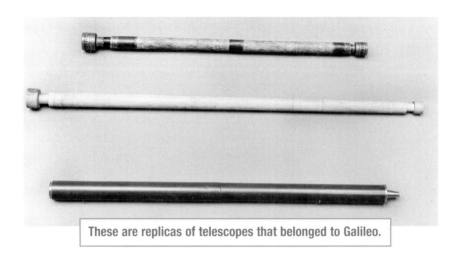

These are replicas of telescopes that belonged to Galileo.

in them. But it was a completely revolutionary instrument at the time, and today it is still the most important tool an astronomer uses. The telescope allowed Galileo to see faint objects that were not visible before. It also showed him nearby objects much more clearly than anyone had ever seen them. Using his new "eyes," he made many discoveries. Galileo realized that no one else had ever seen the details he could see through his telescope. So he looked carefully at every object he studied and made many detailed drawings of them. He saw that the Moon did not have a smooth surface, as everyone had always thought. He could see that it is covered with *craters,* craggy mountains, hills, and broad valleys. Galileo was the first to notice that Venus has phases, as does the Moon. That is, as Earth and Venus both move around the Sun, we sometimes see just a sliver of the Sun's light along one side of Venus's rounded surface. Sometimes we see a half-round of light, while the rest of the planet is in shadow. And sometimes we see the entire *disk*—the flat-looking circle we see from Earth—shining in the full reflected light of the Sun.

With his telescope, Galileo could see the craters on the Moon.

Galileo discovered the four largest moons of Jupiter, which are known today as the Galilean satellites: Io, Europa, Ganymede, and Callisto. It was the first time anyone realized that the other planets also had moons orbiting them. He also noticed a strange bump on each side of Saturn's disk. He was puzzled, but scientists later learned that these bumps were actually an enormous system of rings that circles this giant planet. Galileo recognized that the cloudy light of the Milky Way was actually a vast stream of stars—distinct points of light that no one had ever seen before. He was also the first to study sunspots on the Sun— dark, stormy areas that appear from time to time in the outer, gassy

NASA put together this photo of Jupiter and its four largest moons—Io, Europa, Ganymede, and Callisto.

regions of the Sun. (*Warning:* Never look directly at the Sun. The Sun's rays can seriously damage your eyes and can even cause blindness.)

In the years following Galileo's observations, many lens makers, or opticians, fashioned bigger and better telescopes. In the early days of sky-watching, simple lenses tended to distort images. Lens makers had difficulty grinding perfectly smooth curves to produce flawless glass lenses. Each lens had to be ground by hand, and precision was practically impossible. Large pieces of glass are also heavy and tend to sag. They don't sag a lot—just enough to distort an image. Some astronomers grew concerned with the problems of making lenses more perfect.

In 1663, a Scottish mathematician named James Gregory (1638–75) invented another type of telescope. He knew that a large, smooth mirror was much easier to make than was a perfect lens. Also, because a mirror's job is done on just one side of the glass, the side the light bounces off, the other side could be supported by a frame to reduce sagging. This kind of support could not be used with a lens because light has to shine *through* a lens. A few years later, in 1668, English physicist and astronomer Isaac Newton (1642–1727) made the first successful *reflector,* or reflecting, telescope using mirrors.

From then on, telescopes just got bigger and bigger, increasing their ability to gather light. The more light a telescope could gather, the more the observer could see. You can think of a telescope as a big "light bucket." The lenses and mirrors gather the light and pass it on to the eyepiece.

Over time, artisans became more skilled at fashioning and polishing the mirrors and lenses used by telescopes. In the process, the *optics* (the lenses and mirrors) passed on far more accurate images to the observer.

In the eighteenth century, the English amateur astronomer William Herschel (1738–1822) built a huge reflecting telescope with a mirror 4 feet (1.2 meters) in *diameter* and a tube 40 feet (12 m) long. When asked about the unusual structure of his telescope, Herschel would explain that he was not only after magnification, but he also wanted light-gathering capability. The larger the telescope's mirror, the more light it was capable of capturing from faint objects in the sky. The more light the telescope captured, the more clearly he could see the stars and *nebulae* (Latin for "mist," because they looked like misty clouds) against the dark skies.

Creating and polishing a mirror that size was quite a job, and Herschel had no special equipment for the task. He and his sister, Caroline, set to work in the basement of the Herschel home. They poured a molten mixture of tin and other metals into a mold that, according to legend, was made from horse manure. Then they ground the hardened metal into a parabola. Finally, they made it bright and shiny by polishing it for weeks—a job they had to repeat every few days because the tin mixture quickly blackened with tarnish. The telescope was so large that Herschel had to build a scaffold to hold it. He had to climb a ladder to observe the skies. The effort paid off, though. Looking through his own telescope, Herschel discovered the planet Uranus in 1781. It was the first planet ever observed that ancient people had not already seen and named. Later in his career, Herschel also discovered two of Uranus's moons, as well as two moons of Saturn. Using his immense telescope, he also discovered many clusters and galaxies of stars and approximately 2,400 nebulae.

Herschel's large telescope allowed the great astronomer to probe deeper into space. "I have looked farther into space than ever [a]

Because Galileo's telescope used lenses to produce an image, it is known as a refracting telescope, or *refractor*. In a refractor, light rays from an object pass through a large, main lens, called the *primary objective,* or primary lens. This lens is *convex* (thicker in the middle than at the edges). The shape of the lens bends, or refracts, the light so that it comes together at a focal point behind which a small, upside-down image of the object appears. The eyepiece at the end of the tube, which consists of one or more small lenses, magnifies this image so that the observer can see it more easily.

In a reflecting telescope, or *reflector*, the objective is not a lens. Instead it is a large mirror, called the primary mirror. The shape is curved, or *concave,* so its center appears to be scooped out like a bowl. Light from an object reflects off this mirror and then may be reflected off a secondary mirror. From there, the light bounces back to the eyepiece. The secondary mirror may be flat, convex, or concave. The shape depends on the way the telescope designer wants the light to travel through the telescope. Finally, the image is magnified by the lenses of the eyepiece. Sometimes a camera takes the place of the eyepiece. The *Hubble Space Telescope* is a reflector.

Reflectors may also use an additional small, flat mirror to bend the light. This allows the viewer to see the image from an eyepiece at the side of the telescope, a design still used by many small reflecting telescopes. They are known as Newtonian telescopes in honor of Isaac Newton, who first came up with this design.

Very large observatory telescopes may also have special mechanisms for allowing observers to see through the eyepiece. Sometimes astronomers use an elevator to reach a special cage or platform high up on the telescope just below the observatory dome and near the primary objective. The means used to obtain images from the *Hubble Space Telescope,* though, are even more complicated than that!

This is a photo of an engraving of Isaac Newton's reflecting telescope, known as a Newtonian telescope.

William Herschel looks through the telescope that he and his sister, Caroline, built.

human being did before me," he once wrote. Herschel's first love was the pursuit of the starry realm. And his giant telescope allowed him to peer into its depths.

Herschel's telescope would not remain the biggest, though. Another master builder, Lord Rosse (William Parsons, 3rd Earl of Rosse, 1800–67) from Ireland, built an even bigger telescope in 1844. It was known as the Leviathan of Birr Castle. Its 72-inch (1.8-m) mirror held the record as the largest for nearly a century. The Leviathan remained the world's largest telescope until 1917, when the 100-inch (2.5-m) Hooker telescope was built at Mount Wilson Observatory, northwest of Los Angeles, California. The Hale telescope at neighboring Palomar Observatory set a new record thirty-one years later. The Hale, completed in 1948, measured 200 inches (5 m). At the time, it was by far the largest telescope in the world.

In October 1996 the newly built Keck II telescope on Mauna Kea in Hawaii became the largest reflecting telescope in the world. Its primary mirror is a giant 400 inches, or 33 feet (10 m), in diameter. With this enormous size, the Keck II can gather four times as much light as the Hale telescope. In fact, it can gather seventeen times as much light as the *Hubble Space Telescope!* It can also see farther than the *Hubble*— but not as clearly.

Refracting telescopes are still very popular with amateurs, but as observatory telescopes got bigger, fewer and fewer were the refractor type. Large glass lenses are much heavier than mirrors and are more difficult to make. The largest refractor in the world is the 40-inch (1-m) telescope at Yerkes Observatory in Williams Bay, Wisconsin. It has been in operation since 1897.

Keck I (left) and Keck II are located at the Mauna Kea observatory in Hawaii. Each telescope uses a mirror with a diameter of 10 meters to focus light.

Why a Telescope in Space?

Since the time of Galileo, telescopes have revolutionized astronomy. Bigger and better telescopes on the mountaintops of the world have helped astronomers see much farther and more clearly than ever before. In the four hundred years since telescopes were first invented, astronomers have used them to make enormous discoveries about the solar system and the rest of the universe.

Yet ground-based telescopes—those that reside on Earth's surface—have four frustrating problems: Earth's cloud cover, the turbulence of the atmosphere, the inability of some forms of radiation to penetrate the atmosphere, and light pollution.

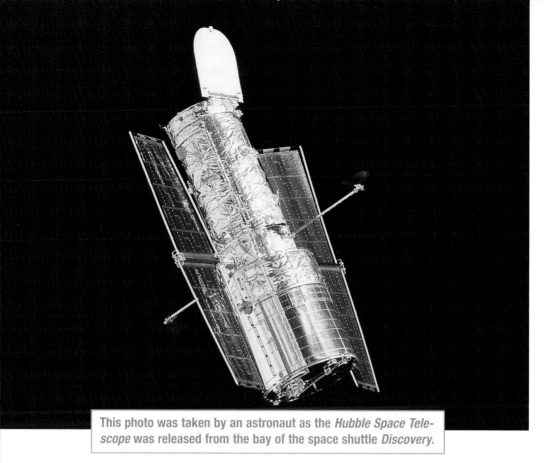

This photo was taken by an astronaut as the *Hubble Space Telescope* was released from the bay of the space shuttle *Discovery*.

- **Cloud Cover.** If you've ever wanted to see an eclipse of the Moon on a cloudy night, you know how frustrating clouds can be for any astronomer. Behind that veil of clouds you know that exciting events are taking place, yet there's nothing you can do but wait and hope the skies clear before the excitement is over. Imagine how unhappy you would be if you were an astronomer and the night arrived when you were scheduled to use one of the few big telescopes that could do your kind of work, and then it turned out to be a cloudy night!

- **Twinkle, Twinkle.** Remember the little rhyme you learned as a kid? "Twinkle, twinkle, little star . . ." Well, twinkling stars are charming, but when you're trying to see how big they are, how luminous they are, what they are made of, and what their environment is like, that twinkling makes the job very difficult. The cause is the constant turbulence of Earth's atmosphere, the layers of gases that lie like a protective blanket over our planet's surface.

Even on a mountaintop, the atmosphere's agitation causes telescopes to capture blurry and indistinct images. Scientists have learned a lot of tricks with improved optics and computerized image processing to help them deal with this. They can make up for a lot of the problem, but they can't compensate for it completely.

- **Blocked Radiation.** Astronomers have discovered that they can learn a lot about the universe by looking at objects in ways other than through optical telescopes (or capturing images with film or electronics). Objects in the universe put out many kinds of radiation that span the range of the *electromagnetic spectrum* (the full range of waves and frequencies of electromagnetic radiation). By using special instruments, scientists can reveal the presence of radiation that would not be detectable with an optical telescope, which looks only at visible light.

However, certain types of radiation do not ever reach Earth's surface. The chemical composition of Earth's atmosphere prevents *infrared* and *ultraviolet* energy from reaching the ground. Infrared radiation is absorbed by water vapor and carbon dioxide (CO_2) in the air. The atmosphere's ozone absorbs ultraviolet rays. Air molecules scatter *X-rays* and *gamma rays,* so they are not easily observed from below Earth's blanket of atmosphere. Telescopes set atop high mountains, flown in high-altitude airplanes, or sent aloft on balloons can visualize more of these types of radiation, but not all of them.

- **Polluting the Darkness.** Most people don't think of light as a kind of pollution. But for astronomers, the lights from city streetlights, stores, homes, and headlights all compete against the tiny, faint objects they are trying to observe. Even the atmosphere itself has a faint, natural glow.

Dreams of Seeing from Space

The regions of space beyond Earth's atmosphere are different. All types of radiation travel through the vacuum of space at the speed of light. There are no clouds. There are no competing lights, except light from celestial objects, including the Sun's direct light and its light that is reflected by the Moon and Earth. There is no atmospheric turbulence in space. There is just the vast vacuum and darkness of space.

As early as 1920, pioneer rocket engineer Hermann Oberth (1894–1989) of Transylvania put forth the idea of a space-based telescope in a popular science article. In 1946, American astronomer Lyman Spitzer (1914–97) wrote a paper that expanded on the idea. Besides the advantages for observation, he noted that the distortion of a telescope's optics by the pull of *gravity* would not be a problem in a space telescope. He suggested using both small and large telescopes. Smaller telescopes—with diameters less than 16.4 feet (5 m)—could examine dust and gases in the areas between the stars (*interstellar* regions). They could also find out what stars are made of. Larger telescopes—between 16.4 and 49.2 feet (5 and 15 m)—could find out more about some of the universe's more mysterious objects, such as globular clusters and galaxies. Perhaps they could also measure the size of the universe.

Science at Work: Using the Electromagnetic Spectrum

The light we see is just a small part of an important family of energies known as the electromagnetic spectrum. Visible light is just about in the middle of the spectrum and we describe it in the different colors of the rainbow. White light (sunlight and starlight) is a mixture of many of these colors. The rest of the electromagnetic spectrum is made up of types of radiation that humans cannot see, yet you will find many of the names of this radiation familiar.

Radio waves and infrared rays occur at one end of the spectrum. Their wavelengths are longer than red light waves, which have the longest wavelengths visible to humans. At the other end of the spectrum are types of radiation with such short wavelengths that they are also invisible to humans, including ultraviolet waves, X-rays, and gamma rays.

Some of this radiation cannot penetrate Earth's atmosphere. So telescopes on Earth's surface are not well suited to "view" these wavelengths emitted by objects in space.

From its position above the atmosphere, though, the *Hubble Space Telescope* can get a clear view. It uses all its instruments to measure radiation levels in different regions of the spectrum. Very cool objects give off infrared waves, although they may emit very little radiation of other types. So scanning the skies for infrared radiation can reveal very cool objects that might otherwise not be detected using conventional, visible-light telescopes. Ultraviolet radiation is given off by very hot and exotic types of sky objects, such as white dwarf stars, planetary nebulae, and explosive phenomena. The *Hubble Space Telescope* can see these objects as well.

Electromagnetic Spectrum

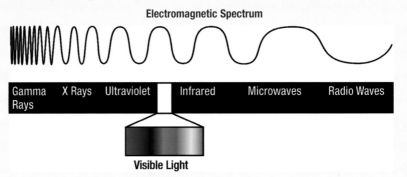

Spitzer was a visionary. He proposed having a major study done of these possibilities in a report written more than ten years before the first satellite was put into *orbit!* Most people at that time thought rockets

Early Space Telescopes

Telescope	Dates of Operation	Description
ORBITING ASTRONOMICAL OBSERVATORY (OAO)	1972–1973	Carried UV telescopes, photoelectric telescopes, and UV spectrometers
COPERNICUS	1972–1981	Part of the OAO series; carried X-ray and UV telescopes
INTERNATIONAL ULTRAVIOLET EXPLORER (IUE)	1978–1996	Established a record of UV sources and took more than 10,000 spectra of objects in its long lifetime
INFRARED ASTRONOMICAL SURVEY (IRAS)	1983	First satellite built to do a major survey at infrared wavelengths
ROENTGEN SATELLITE (ROSAT)	1990	German satellite that carried X-ray and extreme-UV telescopes
EXTREME ULTRAVIOLET EXPLORER (EUVE)	1992–2001	Took a detailed look at the extreme-UV sky
INFRARED SPACE OBSERVATORY (ISO)	1995–1997	A European supplement and replacement for IRAS

and spaceships were only a vague possibility that might become realities in the far-distant future. Some even believed they were no more real than the science-fiction stories portrayed in the movies.

Dawning Possibility

By 1957 the Union of Soviet Socialist Republics (USSR or Soviet Union)—a union of Russia, Belarus, Kazakhstan, and other countries in western Asia and Eastern Europe—had placed a little satellite called *Sputnik* in orbit. Within just three months, the United States com-

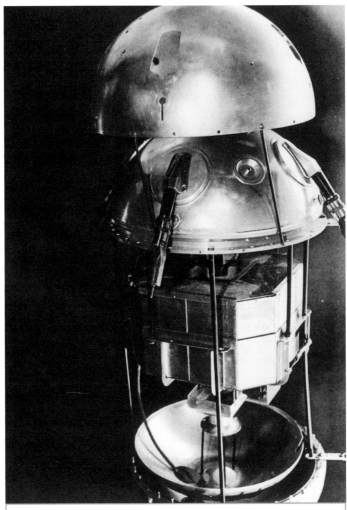

This is a photo of *Sptnik I* before its launch on October 4, 1957.

pleted a rocket and developed, built, and launched its own satellite, named *Explorer 1*—and began to catch up with the Soviets in the space age. In 1958 U.S. President Dwight D. Eisenhower established the National Aeronautics and Space Administration (NASA) to develop and manage programs for exploring space.

By 1972 the first small space telescope, *Copernicus,* was placed in orbit. Its main mirror was 322 inches (82 centimeters) in diameter. Other small telescopes followed, and plans began to develop for something much bigger. By 1990 Spitzer's vision came true with the launch of a large, powerful telescope above the atmosphere—a satellite placed in orbit around Earth known as the *Hubble Space Telescope.*

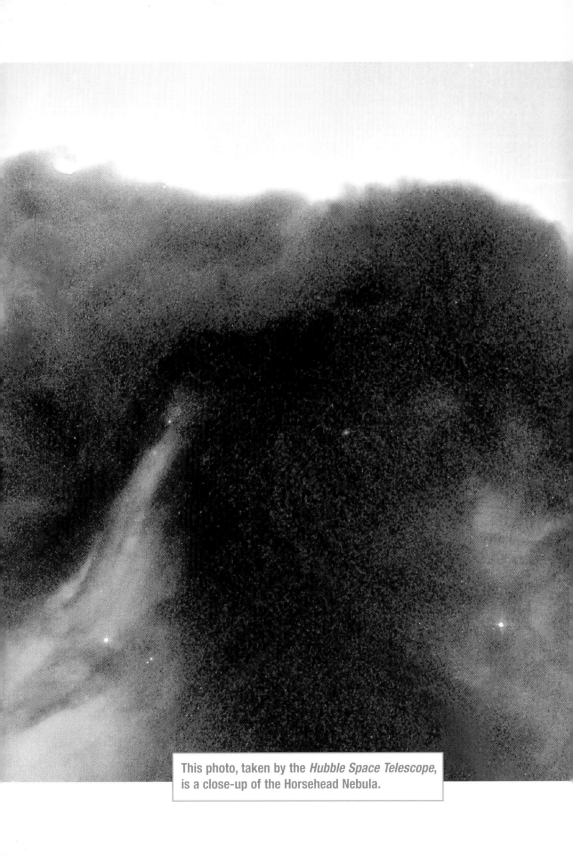

This photo, taken by the *Hubble Space Telescope*, is a close-up of the Horsehead Nebula.

Chapter 2

Hubble's Difficult Journey

By 2000, images from *Hubble's* cameras and instruments appeared daily on the Internet. Astronomy magazines, newsmagazines, and science journals were filled with beautiful and inspiring *Hubble* images. The rest of the world joined astronomers in their wonder at the revelations uncovered by the 2-ton spacecraft. However, the path from Lyman Spitzer's 1946 idea to *Hubble's* orbit above Earth's atmosphere was not an easy one.

By the 1960s, NASA began to take Spitzer's ideas for a large space telescope more seriously. Even the very first U.S. satellite, *Explorer 1,* had demonstrated that a lot could be learned from a spacecraft orbiting Earth. This little cylinder, weighing only 31 pounds (14 kilograms), succeeded in confirming that Earth is surrounded by belts of radiation—now known as the Van Allen belts, after the scientist who designed *Explorer 1*'s experiment.

Spitzer believed that a space telescope could open up a flood of new and astounding information about the universe. He wrote, "The most important contribution of such a radically new and powerful instrument would not be to supplement our current ideas about the universe in which we live, but to uncover new, hitherto unimaginable problems."

By 1969 the United States had succeeded in landing a team of astronauts on the Moon, and NASA had proven its ability to lift heavy loads into Earth's orbit. However, funds for a large space telescope were not yet available. In addition, plans were in the works for a new method for reaching space—a space shuttle. This new vehicle would act as a ferry, shuttling loads into Earth's orbit and then returning to be used again. Up until that time, each spacecraft was used only once. Rockets were built, used, and discarded. The space shuttle would fly again and again and some of its rockets would be reusable.

From the outset the idea of putting a large telescope into orbit was tied to the space shuttle. The shuttle would carry the big telescope into orbit and release it. Then—in the original plan—when it required repairs or upgrades, the shuttle would retrieve it from space and return it to Earth. The shuttle would take the telescope back into orbit after its maintenance visit home.

At shorter intervals, shuttle astronauts could retrieve the telescope for minor patch-ups in the shuttle's cargo bay. They could replace worn parts and update scientific equipment to extend the telescope's life exactly as technicians do at ground-based observatories. There would be one important difference: These repairs would be done in the harsh environment of space as the repair teams floated weightlessly in bulky, pressurized suits.

The plan was complex but seemed like a good one. In 1972 NASA began to develop the shuttle—known as the reusable "space transportation system" (STS). Then official studies for researching and developing the space telescope began in 1975. By 1977 Congress had approved funding for this momentous undertaking.

Some scientists were disappointed by the plans discussed in preliminary studies. The diameter of the mirror would be smaller than many scientists had hoped—only 95 inches (2.4 m). But the important point was that at last a space telescope began to look like a reality. Excitement began to build as the telescope's manufacture began in 1979.

Slowly, Slowly

The mammoth project to build the space telescope involved twenty-one subcontractors, a university, and three NASA centers. Work was done in twenty-one states and twelve countries. The European Space Agency (ESA) was also interested in the idea of a space telescope. ESA agreed to supply the telescope with solar panels, a Faint-Object Camera, and some ground support. In exchange, European astronomers would be allowed a percentage of the observing time in the telescope's schedule.

NASA had a mammoth management job on its hands. As NASA program scientist Nancy Roman remarked at the time, communication was a prime concern. Astronomers knew what kind of telescope they wanted, but they didn't know how to build it. Engineers knew

how to build spacecrafts and telescopes, but no spacecraft or telescope like this one had ever been built. "I felt my job, not only with the space telescope, but with other projects as well, was to keep the two sides talking to each other," Roman said. ". . . I felt I was acting as interpreter between the engineers and the scientists because, while they both wanted the same thing in the end, they didn't speak the same language."

Even once all the pieces of the telescope were completed and assembled and it was safely launched, an army of three hundred people would need to oversee its daily operations.

Almost nothing went smoothly. Delays occurred. Problems loomed. The mirror was more difficult and time-consuming to build than anyone had expected. Yet pressures from Congress and public opinion demanded results. With a project this complex, these demands were unrealistic. In response, NASA had to make choices. The agency allocated more money for the manufacture of the mirror but told the subcontractor to speed up the process. Under pressure, the subcontractor complied. But to meet the new time deadline, some of the time-consuming tests built into the original schedule were not performed. That turned out to be an unfortunate decision.

The 1983 launch date came and went. The telescope was not ready. No one had ever built a civilian satellite like this before. (The military had built telescope satellites but unfortunately did not share its experience!) So new technology had to be developed. The telescope itself had to be different from telescopes that functioned on the ground. Problems arose and took extra time to correct. It was a difficult job, but finally, as 1985 drew to an end, the space telescope was ready. It now also had a name—the *Hubble Space Telescope*—and it was set to launch in 1986.

Grounded

Then tragedy struck. On January 28, 1986, the space shuttle *Challenger* lifted off from its launch pad at Kennedy Space Center. It was the twenty-fifth shuttle flight. Less than two minutes after liftoff, *Challenger* exploded in a fireball. All seven crew members died. The disaster brought all shuttle missions to a complete standstill while investigators probed to find out what had caused the accident and to make sure that it didn't happen again. As it turned out, *Challenger*, like the *Hubble Space Telescope*, had suffered from time pressure and budget cuts. People took too many shortcuts and did too little testing.

For *Challenger*, the problem lay with a sealing ring, known as an O-ring, that did not perform well under extremely cold conditions. On that chilly January morning, rocket fuel leaked around the ring and ignited.

No shuttle launch took place for more than two and a half years. When launches resumed, the schedule was cautious. No one wanted overscheduling to cause another accident. As a result, *Hubble* sat in storage for another five years, waiting its turn to be lifted into orbit.

The crew of the space shuttle *Challenger.*

Launch at Last

Finally, on April 24, 1990, the space shuttle *Discovery* sat on the launch pad, ready for the thirty-fifth shuttle mission. The *Hubble Space Telescope* was safely locked in the shuttle's cargo bay. The giant rockets roared. Steam and smoke filled the air, and the shuttle thundered into the sky. Thousands watched as the NASA announcer commented, " . . . and liftoff of the space shuttle *Discovery* with the *Hubble Space Telescope*—our window on the universe."

Liftoff of the space shuttle *Discovery* on April 24, 1990.

Shortly after entering orbit, *Discovery's* cargo bay doors opened. To avoid any fire hazard, the crew waited for the air inside the telescope to vent into space. Only then did the astronauts receive the go-ahead to turn on the main power switch.

Next, the *Hubble's* ground-control team went through a process to protect the telescope against damage from cold and heat. They turned on thermostats and heaters. Then they checked the health of the spacecraft's computer.

On the second morning of the mission, the shuttle crew turned on *Hubble's* internal power system and disconnected the power supplied by the shuttle. For the next step, astronauts Kathryn Sullivan and Bruce McCandless stood by, suited up in their pressure suits. If *Hubble's* automatic systems had any trouble with the next crucial steps, they were ready to do an emergency space walk to help out.

From the ground, *Hubble* received the signal to unfurl its solar arrays. They stretched out straight and taut, their tawny color bright against the sky. Then, the telescope's six batteries started charging up as the solar cells converted the Sun's energy to electrical power. Next, the two high-gain antennae emerged. These were the keys to communicating with *Hubble* through the Tracking and Data Relay Satellite System (TDRSS). Last, ground control turned on the pointing systems so that scientists and engineers could direct *Hubble* to turn its gaze.

Finally, *Hubble* was ready. The long, remote manipulator arm of the shuttle grappled the bulky satellite and moved it out of the cargo bay, extending out toward the Andes Mountains passing below. There, over South America, the telescope emerged from the shuttle and floated freely as people all over the world watched on television. It was

This photo, taken by the *Remote Manipulator System*, shows the *Hubble Space Telescope* being released into orbit high over South America.

an emotional moment, especially for scientists who had been waiting more than ten years for this moment. Everyone knew that a new adventure—and a new era in astronomy—had just begun.

The *Hubble Space Telescope* floats away from the space shuttle *Discovery* after a servicing mission.

Chapter 3

First Light

The great space observatory had been launched at last. About the size of a railroad car, it looked a lot like a stack of giant silver canisters with wings. Its silvery covering of polyester film glinted in the Sun as the telescope settled into its orbit, hovering above Earth's atmosphere. It was beautiful, exciting, and exhilarating. Soon, astronomers felt confident, this long-awaited beauty would be ready to become the new window to the universe. Soon it would hand them the keys to many mysteries.

First, though, this extremely complex, precise, and sensitive spacecraft would have to go through a long process of testing. Did everything survive the journey? Had the optics, or "eyes"—the mirrors, supporting trusses, and *apertures*—all arrived in orbit safely? Were any of its systems damaged during activation? Was its computer in good shape? How were the communications working? Were of all the telescope's systems up and running? Would engineers and scientists be able to point it as accurately as they needed to? Everything would need to be adjusted and set with precision.

How Does Hubble Do Its Work?

The *Hubble Space Telescope* is composed of three main parts: the spacecraft, the optics, and the instruments. These parts work as a team to make all of *Hubble's* spectacular work possible.

The spacecraft houses the telescope's optics and instruments, protects them from the harsh environment of space, transports them in their rapid journey around Earth, and communicates with home. Inside the spacecraft's protective skin, the telescope itself relies on its optics to gather light and resolve images into distinct details. Ground crews send messages to the onboard instruments to point the telescope toward its targets, guide its functions, and instruct it to carry on its imaging.

Hubble, The Spacecraft

The *Hubble Space Telescope* has some special advantages, but it also has some challenges that ground-based telescopes do not have: It is orbiting Earth at a speed of 17,500 miles (28,164 km) per hour. It has to generate its own power and carry its own computer. It has to have means for observers and investigators on Earth to position and point its apertures. It has to have protection against the extreme cold and heat of space, and it has to have equipment for archiving data and transmitting them to Earth.

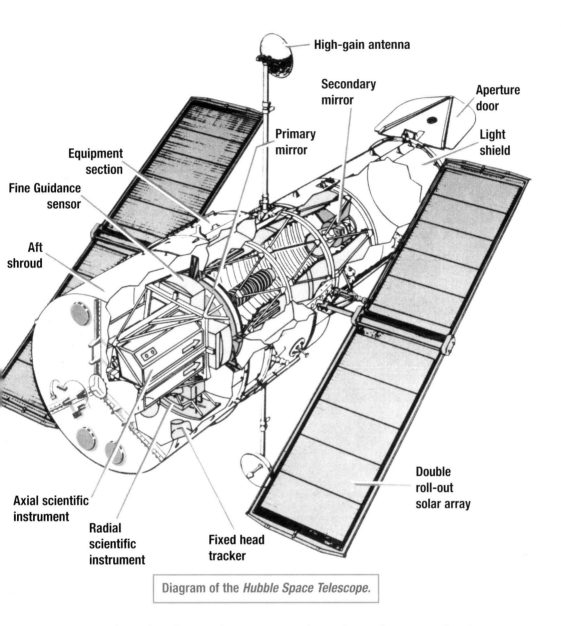

High-gain antenna

Secondary mirror

Aperture door

Primary mirror

Light shield

Equipment section

Fine Guidance sensor

Aft shroud

Axial scientific instrument

Radial scientific instrument

Fixed head tracker

Double roll-out solar array

Diagram of the *Hubble Space Telescope*.

Traveling that fast—whizzing around Earth at about 5 miles (8 km) per second—means that *Hubble*'s delicate instruments are darting in and out of Earth's shadow about once every ninety-five minutes.

The *Hubble Space Telescope*

Vital Statistics

LAUNCH DATE	April 25, 1990
AVERAGE DISTANCE FROM EARTH	381 miles (613 km)
TYPE OF TELESCOPE	Reflector
DIAMETER OF PRIMARY MIRROR	94.4 inches (2.4 m)
MASS	11,600 kg (a weight of 25,575 pounds on Earth)
INSTRUMENTS (AS OF 2001)	Fine Guidance Sensors (FGS) Space Telescope Imaging Spectrograph (STIS) Wide Field/Planetary Camera 2 (WFPC2) Faint Object Camera (FOC) Near Infrared Camera and Multi-Object Spectrometer (NICMOS)
FUTURE INSTRUMENTS	Advanced Camera for Surveys (ACS) Cosmic Origins Spectrograph (COS) Wide-Field Camera 3 (WFC3)
PREVIOUS INSTRUMENTS (LATER UPDATED WITH REPLACEMENTS)	Faint Object Spectrograph (FOS) Goddard High Resolution Spectrograph (GHRS) High-Speed Photometer (HSP) Wide Field/Planetary Camera (WFPC)

The speed is so great that it's like traveling from Washington, D.C., on the East Coast of the United States, to San Francisco, on the West Coast, in just over eight minutes. When Earth blocks the sunlight, temperatures in space dip to extremes far below freezing. Then, a few minutes later, the spacecraft is scorched by sunlight, which raises its surface temperature dramatically. Imagine stepping from a frozen meat locker into the full heat of the Mojave Desert. That's the type of temperature change *Hubble* goes through several times a day. So *Hubble* wears a thermal blanket to keep the temperature steady for the instruments inside.

Meanwhile, *Hubble* also needs power. The spacecraft carries its own means of generating the power needed for its computers, the equipment for pointing the telescope in the right direction, and the instruments that capture the stunning images we see. Two *solar arrays* 40 feet (12.2 m) long and 8 feet (2.4 m) wide take care of that job. These winglike extensions are flexible, lightweight, and flat. Each one holds hundreds of solar cells on its surface to capture the energy of the Sun's rays and convert it to 2,400 watts of electricity—enough to light two dozen household light bulbs. These solar cells not only power all of *Hubble's* systems, but they also charge up a set of batteries that take over when the satellite is passing through Earth's shadow and is out of the sunlight. Out of each ninety-seven-minute orbit, *Hubble* has to run on stored battery power for about thirty-six minutes.

A telescope onboard a spacecraft is far away from the people using it. How do they tell the telescope which way to point, and how do they find out what images the telescope has captured? That's where *Hubble's* communication and archiving systems come in. As *Hubble* travels around Earth, sometimes ground technicians can reach it by radio communications and sometimes they can't. So all of *Hubble's* activities are planned ahead in detail and sent to the spacecraft in batches.

Where does a spacecraft get its power? What runs the many instruments onboard and the computer that receives instructions from home? The energy for most of these activities comes directly from the Sun. The energy is collected in solar cells arranged in groups called solar panels, or solar arrays. They look like huge, flat windmill blades or wings.

Within a solar cell, the energy from sunlight is converted directly into electricity. This process changes photons (particles of solar energy) into electricity (current). A *volt* is one type of electrical unit. So the process is known as the *photovoltaic effect.* The large surface area of the solar panels provides a big area for harvesting, or collecting, the sunlight.

Inside a solar cell are two thin layers of material—commonly silicon—one on top of the other. Before building the solar cell, technicians modify the two layers so that one attracts positive particles and the other attracts negative particles.

As particles flow from the Sun into a solar cell, the cell produces current from some and not from others, depending on whether they are positive or negative. The solar cell produces electricity through a game of Kick the Can, as electrons move in a circuit between the positive and negative layers of material.

Solar cells have been around since the 1950s, when researchers at Bell Laboratories first developed them. You've probably used solar cells on a smaller scale in calculators and wristwatches. They are also used to power equipment in remote areas on Earth where laying electrical cables or wires would be costly. Engineers began using solar arrays for power onboard spacecrafts with the first U.S. satellite, *Explorer 1,* which was launched in 1958. Spacecrafts have been using them ever since.

The *International Space Station* is powered by solar energy.

This task alone is a complex job. Experts at the Space Telescope Science Institute in Maryland write careful, step-by-step instructions. Suppose you walked into the kitchen one morning and found a note on the table that read: "Eat breakfast quickly and Anna will pick you up at 8:30." You would understand what it meant, even though it left out a lot of details. That wouldn't be enough for *Hubble*, though. The instructions would have to include even the most minute steps: Open refrigerator door. Find milk. Grasp carton with hand. Lift up. Pull arm toward body. Close refrigerator door. Turn 180 degrees and walk to table. Set milk down. . . . You get the idea. For *Hubble*, detailed instructions are written in a programming code, which is the language understood by *Hubble*'s computer. Finally, operators at Goddard Space Flight Center, also in Maryland, beam the coded plans up to the spacecraft. New code has to be sent at regular intervals to cover every moment of every day.

Getting a Grip

Once the day's schedule is set, the telescope's pointing systems begin their job. The pointers find the objects on *Hubble*'s list of targets— far-off stars, galaxies, clusters, and planets. Then they lock on to them one by one. This job requires great precision. It's like standing on the Eads Bridge in St. Louis, Missouri, and steadily pointing a laser beam at a spot the size of a postage stamp on a wall in Atlanta, Georgia.

To make an observation, *Hubble* needs to locate a pair of bright stars, called guide stars, near each target it seeks. These bright stars act as *Hubble*'s anchors. Guide stars allow *Hubble* to hold steady on a target. Like a ship anchored in a harbor or a sturdy three-legged stool,

Hubble is steadied by the three-way tension between its position and the two guide stars' positions. As mission planners prepare *Hubble* for each target, they look for anchors for the spacecraft to use. Choosing from a sort of "address book" of fifteen million stars, they can usually find two that have convenient "addresses" for every object they want *Hubble* to photograph.

Hubble also needs to hold steady, which is essential for capturing clear photographs. Like an acrobat on a tightrope, the orbiting observatory needs to keep perfect balance against the forces that fight stability—including drag (from the extremely thin atmosphere that extends into its low orbit), radiation from the Sun, and the gravitational pull of other objects, such as Earth. Sometimes, for imaging faraway or faint objects, *Hubble* needs to use long exposure times. By allowing light to strike the *charge-coupled device,* or *CCD* for long periods, *Hubble* can gather as much light as possible from these objects, which are otherwise too dim to photograph. This may require holding steady for hours. If *Hubble* wobbles even slightly, the images will be blurred.

Luckily the telescope has some expert help—an elaborate pointing control system. A set of *gyroscopes* keeps its attitude steady. (A gyroscope is a device that is set in a frame in such a way that its wheels always bring it back to its original attitude. "Attitude" is not a hostile state of mind in this case—it's the position of an object horizontally and vertically in relation to a reference object, such as a horizon or star.) After *Hubble* has locked onto a target object, the gyroscopes' Fine Guidance Sensors (FGS) check constantly for movement away from the target. If the FGS detect movement, they initiate smooth speed changes in the gyroscope wheels to make an even transition back to the locked position.

Optics

Hubble's position above the atmosphere removes most obstacles to clear vision. But the telescope needs more than that to obtain clean, crisp, razor-sharp photos. It needs superior optics, which consist of a combination of two mirrors, braces to support the mirrors, and the instrument apertures. The pieces of this system provide *Hubble*'s "eye." The two mirrors are mounted in a system called the Ritchey-Chretien Cassegrain. This system allows the largest possible field of view.

Light travels through a special tube in the telescope that is designed to keep stray light out. Then it reflects off the primary mirror, which is concave. The reflected light bounces straight back to a smaller, secondary mirror. This mirror is convex. The light reflects off the secondary mirror, through an opening in the primary mirror, to a point of focus. There, the focused image is picked up by the scientific instruments, such as the Faint Object Camera.

The quality of these mirrors has to be very high. They must be ground to a precise curve. They are made from special materials that resist expanding or shrinking in response to changes in temperature. The demanding specifications call for a surface so smooth and perfectly curved that even if the mirror were much larger—say, having a diameter equal to Earth's—no bump on its surface would be more than 6 inches (15.2 cm) high.

Snapping the Pictures

Hubble is designed to excel in visible-light photography. It also carries instruments that allow near-infrared and near-ultraviolet observations, so it can capture invisible radiation just beyond visible violet and visible red. Several of NASA's other satellite observatories complement

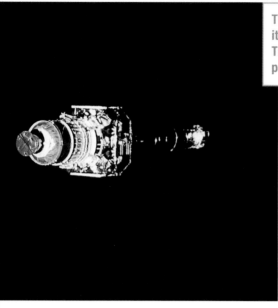

The *Chandra X-ray Observatory* shortly after its release from the space shuttle *Columbia*. The *Chandra X-ray Observatory* is the most powerful X-ray telescope.

Hubble by capturing images in other regions of the spectrum. The *Chandra X-ray Observatory* takes images of X-ray radiation in the universe. And before its retirement in 2000, the *Compton Gamma Ray Observatory* focused on highly energetic gamma-ray emissions.

Hubble carries numerous scientific instruments that act as astronomers' eyes into the skies. On Earth, an astronomer can usually look through a telescope's lens and see objects in the nighttime sky. With *Hubble,* though, a scientist can't do that. So *Hubble's* instruments do the job for astronomers. Of course, *Hubble* carries cameras. But the space-borne observatory does not carry film. Instead, it records images on a chip known as a charge-coupled device (CCD).

As *Hubble* floated out of the cargo bay that April day in 1990, it carried two cameras. One was a Wide Field and Planetary Camera (WFPC). This workhorse camera is the source of most of *Hubble's* most famous pictures. *Hubble's* photo of the Eagle Nebula is one of the WFPC's best-known pictures. The camera has forty-eight filters that allow it to be sensitive to many different wavelengths of electromagnetic radiation, ranging from ultraviolet to visible light to near infrared. The second camera was the Faint Object Camera. Similar to

A CCD is a very sensitive surface mounted on a silicon chip. Its eyesight is 1 billion times keener than the naked human eye and is capable of discerning extraordinarily faint objects. It is especially designed to capture light images electronically by converting light intensity into current. Special software translates the images into clear, digital data that can be transmitted through radio communications. The images often show much finer detail than images recorded on either photographic plates or film.

These high-quality digital pictures are also much easier to store. This is important because scientists can make use of the images stored in the *Hubble* archives for many decades. Already, astronomers all over the world obtain between ten and fifty *gigabytes* (billions of bytes) of data every day from *Hubble*'s archive (the library, or database, on Earth where the digital images are stored). This steady supply of stunning new images will fuel thousands of papers in the years to come. (More than 2,500 scientific papers based on the first ten years of *Hubble* images have been published by astronomers.)

a telephoto lens, this camera has extremely high *resolution*—that is, it can capture very detailed images in a small area.

Hubble also had two *spectrographs* onboard. These instruments work something like a prism, separating starlight into its rainbow of colors. Astronomers can figure out a star's temperature, motion, age, and composition by using a spectrograph to study the light radiated by the star.

These scientific instruments provide the means for collecting data from the reflecting mirrors. The data are then sent back to Earth by the satellite's communication system.

Keeping in Touch

In spite of all the powerful instruments aboard *Hubble,* nothing would happen without the help of a healthy communications system. *Hubble* is a robot—it's sophisticated, but it needs instructions. It does only what it's told.

Hubble is also constantly gathering information, but those images would do no one any good if they were stuck onboard the satellite. In its first ten years of scanning the skies, *Hubble* collected 3.5 *terabytes* (trillion *bytes*) of data, and every day it gathers enough to fill up half the hard drive of the average home computer (3 to 5 gigabytes). All this information is useless unless it can be sent to Earth for people to use. The communications antennae and a relay system keep the channels open.

The communications antennae ensure that the ground crews and astronomers can keep the telescope informed about what to do and when to do it. *Hubble* has four antennae for sending and receiving information to and from the Space Telescope Operations Control Center at NASA's Goddard Space Flight Center.

However, as *Hubble* orbits, it sometimes moves out of view, or "earshot," of Goddard. So scientists use a relay to communicate with the telescope through the TDRSS. This system of satellites provides "listening posts" in different locations above Earth's surface, so *Hubble* is usually in a direct line of sight with one of

SPACE TELESCOPE

After *Hubble* takes the picture, the image is sent to the TDRSS satellite which sends the image to the TDRSS terminal in New Mexico. From there, the image is sent to Goddard Space Flight Center. Once the images are stored and reviewed, they are sent other places. In this case, the image was sent to the Science Institute in Baltimore, Maryland.

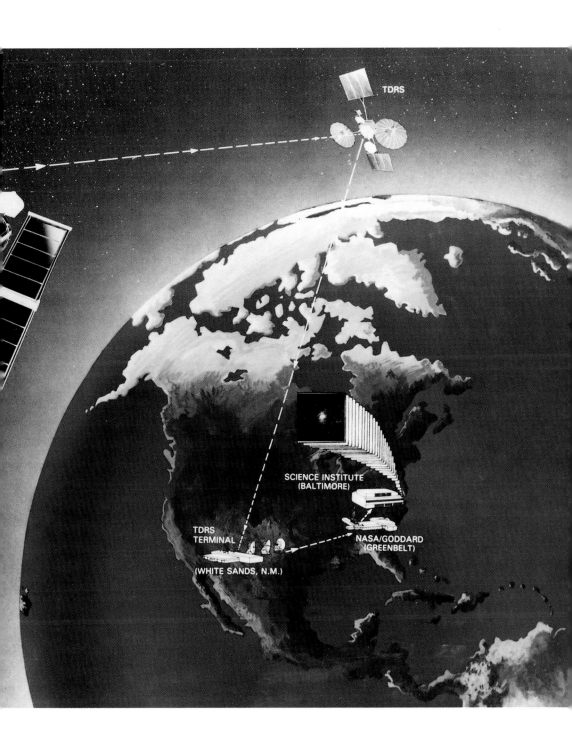

TDRS

SCIENCE INSTITUTE
(BALTIMORE)

TDRS
TERMINAL

(WHITE SANDS, N.M.)

NASA/GODDARD
(GREENBELT)

them. The TDRSS then sends the information to giant antennae on the ground. Otherwise, the spacecraft stores its data and transmits them later, when one of the relay satellites is back in view.

First Light

This was the complex system of modular instruments and equipment that made up the telescope that was placed in orbit in April 1990. The space shuttle *Discovery* moved away from *Hubble* slowly to avoid contaminating the carefully preserved spotlessness of the telescope's optics with outgassing, water vapor, or other emissions. But the shuttle stayed within the neighborhood for a couple of days, just in case *Hubble* needed help.

Of course, a few problems did turn up in those first few days. The system was so complex, though, that no one was really surprised. The front cover of the telescope failed to open on signal, and the telescope put itself in safe mode, a self-protective semisleep. Once safe mode is triggered, the computers are programmed to ignore routine instructions from the outside. They point the telescope away from the dangerous rays of the Sun, position the solar panels to receive the light they need to generate power, and just wait. It took a while to coax the satellite out of safe mode—and it would not be the last time in the telescope's lifetime that safe mode would kick in.

The next problem, though, was more serious. As the satellite passed from sunlight to shadow during each orbit, the solar arrays trembled. The change in temperature seemed to be warping the vast, winglike blades. The trembling was so extreme that the gyroscopes did not always keep the spacecraft in proper orientation. The flight controllers and programmers focused on finding a way to regain control.

Nearly a month had gone by and still no images had been taken. Finally, on May 20, 1990, astronomers prepared for the exciting moment they called "first light"—the moment when the first rays of light would enter the telescope's aperture and *Hubble*'s WFPC would capture an image. At last they would see the universe through the new eyes of *Hubble*.

Disappointment

The excitement quickly changed to concern, though. The first few images seemed okay at first. The camera and the optics appeared to be working. But something seemed strange. A smudge or blur appeared in the center of each image. In images of bright stars, appendages seemed to sprout from the blur, making it look like a stellar spider. Picture after picture had the same problem.

Scientist thought that the blur might be caused by a problem with the WFPC. So they tried using the FOC, but their hearts sank. The same flaw appeared in those images as well. The problem was with the optics themselves. It was the mirror—one of the few components of the space telescope that could not be replaced by a quick exchange in the shuttle's cargo bay.

What could be done? Bring the telescope home and mount a new mirror? This was not really possible. It had become clear that *Hubble* would not survive the stresses of a return to Earth. That plan had to be thrown out. A return to Earth would also probably contaminate the telescope.

For a while, it looked as if the entire mission might be scrapped. Things came to a standstill. Luckily, the subcontractor that built the mirror still had the test site set up. A team of experts reviewed the test

Technicians wear masks and special suits to maintain absolute cleanliness when working on the *Hubble*'s primary mirror.

procedure and discovered where they had gone wrong. They sharpened their pencils and began figuring.

Scientists discovered the issue. Even though the mirror was flawed, it was correctly ground, but the curve was slightly wrong. The primary mirror was 2 microns (2 millionths of a meter) too flat at the edge. Engineers figured out how to correct for this error and devised a package that could take the place of one of the instruments in the stacked canisters that made up the telescope. The device was called COSTAR

(Corrective Optics Space Telescope Axial Replacement). It provided additional mirrors that were ground to create the exact opposite effect of the defective primary mirror. Together, it was hoped that they would produce a perfect image.

COSTAR would take the place of the High-Speed Photometer (HSP), which was one of the original onboard instruments. The swap would have to wait, though, until 1993, when a shuttle mission could be scheduled. Until then, scientists could still use the two onboard spectrographs. Because the spectrographs are not optical instruments, they could continue to function perfectly, unaffected by the flawed mirror.

They did, and the spectrographs made several important observations, including the discovery of a new, giant, white spot that had formed in the clouds of Saturn. Astronomers also spotted a possible planetary nursery around the star Beta Pictoris and emissions from the supernova 1987A. They also observed a strange formation described as the "Einstein Cross," a magnification of a quasar seen through several galaxies that create a sort of gravitational lens. The telescope took more than forty-five thousand images and provided research for some thousand astronomers. Though crippled, *Hubble* proved that it could still produce useful data.

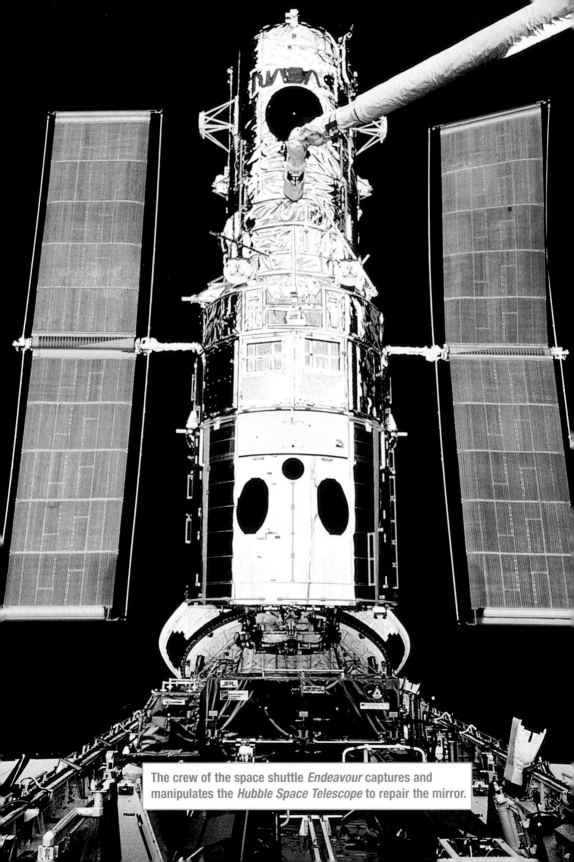

The crew of the space shuttle *Endeavour* captures and manipulates the *Hubble Space Telescope* to repair the mirror.

4

Have Wrench, Will Orbit

The pressure was on for NASA. The *Hubble Space Telescope* was one of the biggest projects to have been undertaken by the agency since Project Apollo, which had taken astronauts to the Moon and back. The mission to fix the space telescope had to succeed. Officially, NASA administrators preferred to think of this mission as a routine "servicing mission," not a repair mission. But, of course, everyone knew it wasn't really routine.

The problem with the mirror was a huge disappointment. Although confident that COSTAR could fix the problem, engineers who tested the package found that, even with COSTAR, some images would not come in as clearly as everyone had hoped. Their tests showed that the precise brightness of a faint star against a very faint background could not be determined. So plans for observing pulsating stars in other galaxies would have to be abandoned until later.

Of course, the flaw in the mirror was actually very small—a difference of less than 2 percent of the breadth of a human hair. Yet, when astronomers examined images closely, the errors became all too apparent.

Seven Ace Space Mechanics

On December 2, 1993, seven astronauts set out on one of the most difficult missions ever undertaken in the history of NASA. The shuttle crew included Dick Covey as commander and Kenneth Bowersox as pilot. Their challenge was to meet up with *Hubble* in orbit. Then two teams of two mission specialists each would alternate in five space walks—a record at the time. The pressure was intense, not only because NASA needed this mission to succeed, but also because the quarters were cramped inside the *Hubble* and the equipment the crew would be handling was delicate. Worst of all, if astronauts lost so much as a screw inside *Hubble,* they could be responsible for ruining the mirror beyond any usefulness.

NASA sent a team of experts. Veteran Story Musgrave had served as an astronaut since 1967. He had already flown on four previous shuttle missions. (At the same time, he earned a master's degree in literature to round out his other academic degrees in mathematics and statistics, operations analysis and computer programming, chemistry, medicine, and physiology and biophysics.) He and his EVA (extra vehicular activity, or space walk) partner, Jeffrey Hoffman, would take the first shift.

The second shift would be handled by Kathryn Thornton and Tom Akers, who had worked together before, repairing the handicapped *INTELSAT 6* communications satellite in May 1992. Inside the shuttle, mission specialist Claude Nicollier would use the robot manipulator arm to assist the spacewalkers by helping them move bulky pieces. The robot arm also served as a base of operations when the astronauts needed it.

The members of the repair crew had the combined experience of sixteen previous shuttle missions. They also had each spent more than one thousand hours in training for the complex mission before them. Much of that time was spent underwater, where buoyancy created effects similar to the effects of weightlessness in space. There they practiced using the skills they would need for performing repairs during space walks onboard the *Endeavour*.

Their job was cut out for them. In addition to the main purpose of their mission—installing the COSTAR package to correct the flaw in the mirror—they had several other difficult maintenance projects to perform. They would also replace two gyroscopes that had worn out, remove *Hubble's* damaged solar arrays and replace them with new ones, and install a new wide-field camera, which would compensate for the flawed mirror for that instrument. In addition, they would perform several maintenance chores.

Once Nicollier had snared *Hubble* with the robot arm and set it in the shuttle's cargo bay, Covey gave this happy report to mission control: "Houston, *Endeavour* has a firm handshake with Mr. Hubble's telescope."

The next job was to replace the worn gyroscopes in order to keep *Hubble* balanced. This took priority over updating the instruments, since the whole project could be in jeopardy if the gyroscopes were not fixed. Musgrave and Hoffman spent most of the first night replacing the ailing gyroscopes so that *Hubble* could keep its balance. The process went smoothly, but it took long hours and both astronauts

When Kathryn "K.T." Thornton was growing up in Montgomery, Alabama, she never imagined that she would ever be an astronaut. All the astronauts at that time were men, and there were very few, even of them. She says that her mother never discouraged her from any of her goals, though, and times changed. After she received her Ph.D. in physics from the University of Virginia in 1979, she was selected by NASA to become an astronaut.

Thornton has flown on the space shuttle four times, and each time the challenges have been different. During an Internet question-and-answer session in 1996, she remarked, "I think the neatest thing about being an astronaut, aside from the opportunity to fly in space, is that I got to continue to learn new things. Every mission was different and required learning to do new things."

Her first mission, STS-33 in November 1989, was a classified mission for the Department of Defense—that is, the military has not released further details. Her second flight was aboard STS-49, the initial test flight of the orbiter *Endeavour* in May 1992. During STS-49, she performed a space walk to test out techniques that would later be used for assembling the International Space Station.

Thornton's third flight, STS-63 in December 1993, sent her out on another EVA to help replace the bent solar panels on the *Hubble Space Telescope* and install the COSTAR corrective optics package. One of her jobs involved hanging onto one of the old, damaged solar panels while the orbiter *Endeavour* sped around Earth at 17,500 miles (28,163.5 km) per hour. (Of course, onboard the shuttle, this tremendous speed is not really noticeable!) Then she had to toss it overboard at just the right moment.

Thornton's final mission, STS-73, took place in November 1995 aboard the orbiter *Columbia*. On this flight, she was payload commander of the second United States Microgravity Laboratory mission. She was honored in 1999, along with six other female astronauts, for her courage by the Explorers Club, a professional society of explorers and researchers.

More recently, Thornton has become the assistant dean for graduate programs at the University of Virginia. She says she would like to see one of her students have the opportunity to walk on Mars. She highly recommends the job of astronaut. Her sparkling sense of humor emerges as she gives this job description: "Astronaut: Looking for excitement, challenges,

were tense and breathing heavily. At one point, with his feet anchored to the robot arm, Hoffman lowered Musgrave upside-down into the telescope—a novel way to do the job. Of course, Musgrave's blood didn't rush to his head, because in space, there is no up or down.

around the world travel? Prepared for long hours, hard work, and extensive on-the-job training? Do you enjoy learning new things? Would you like to be a member of one of the largest and most successful teams in the world? Pay is okay but other compensations are out of this world. Applications accepted at NASA, Johnson Space Center Astronaut Selection Office, Houston, Texas 77058."

Astronaut Kathryn Thorton services the *Hubble Space Telescope*.

Musgrave and Hoffman had successfully replaced the gyroscopes, but then Hoffman muttered, "Uh-oh, we're in trouble." The gyroscopes were located behind a set of doors onboard the satellite. They had opened with no problem, but now, with the job finished, he and

Musgrave could not get them to latch closed. Apparently, the temperature change had caused them to warp, or expand just enough so they would not close completely. Leaving them unlatched, though, was not an option on this big, expensive piece of equipment. The two tried every trick they could think of. But in space, every movement is in slow motion. You can't just bang on a door or slam your body against it to get it to shut. So Musgrave braced himself against the robot arm for leverage and pushed as hard as he could against the doors. Finally, he got them shut. The first space walk ended, and it was a success.

It was too soon to celebrate, though. The next EVA brought more challenges. The following night, Akers and Thornton took on the solar panel replacement. They removed the old, bent panels, but one of them would not roll up. So Akers handed the mangled panel to Thornton, who rode on the robot arm to the edge of the cargo bay and tipped the panel overboard to orbit on its own, flapping in the exhaust from the space shuttle's engines.

The main project for the third night was the installation of the new Wide-Field and Planetary Camera 2. Sporting corrected optics, this camera, the size of a baby grand piano, would replace the old Wide-Field and Planetary Camera. One wrong move and the camera's mirror could be ruined, so the going was tense, but the Musgrave and Hoffman team succeeded with this job, too.

Thornton and Akers took on the task of installing COSTAR, the corrective optics package that would fix the telescope's flawed primary mirror. COSTAR would correct the flawed mirror's effects on the Faint Object Camera—*Hubble's* most powerful instrument. This package was not small, either. It had a mass of 290 kilograms (a weight of 640 pounds on Earth) and was about the size of a telephone booth.

It contained ten mirrors that folded out like blades on a pocketknife. The job took seven hours to complete.

Finally, Musgrave and Hoffman wrapped up the last of the job with some housekeeping tasks—making sure everything was latched up, replacing covers at the top of the telescope, and unfurling the new solar panels. Finally they were done, and using the robot arm, Nicollier set *Hubble* back into orbit.

The crew of seven ace astronaut-mechanics received a jubilant call from President Bill Clinton and Vice President Al Gore. "You made it look easy," Clinton told them. It was a job well done.

Four weeks later, NASA succeeded in confirming what everyone had hoped: The new "eyeglasses" worked. *Hubble*'s vision was repaired, and the new pictures it took were clear and beautiful. The repair crew "mechanics" were heroes.

New Stuff for Hubble

By 1993 *Hubble* had made an impressive list of contributions to astronomy. It looked more deeply into the universe than ever before and its gaze revealed thousands of galaxies. It also allowed astronomers to trace the evolution of the universe. It contributed evidence that most of the stars in the universe formed long, long ago. It gave scientists evidence about the nature and location of quasars and black holes.

By February 1997, though, it was time for another service call to check up on the telescope's health. The space shuttle *Discovery* carried a new team of astronauts, trained especially for the jobs to be done. (Only Commander Kenneth Bowersox, pilot on the first *Hubble* repair flight, was brought in from the first repair team.) This crew's primary mission was to install updated instruments to make the space telescope's

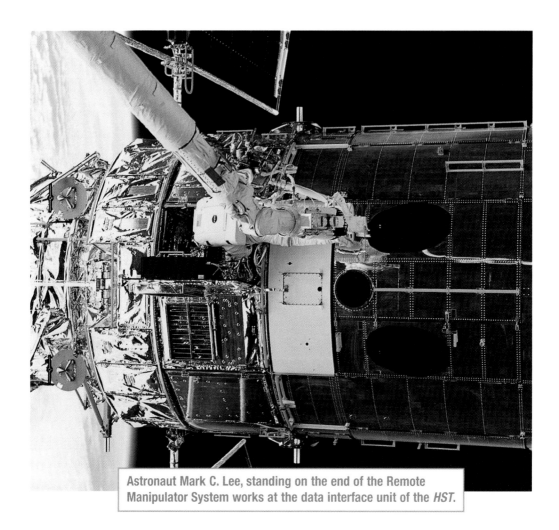

Astronaut Mark C. Lee, standing on the end of the Remote Manipulator System works at the data interface unit of the *HST*.

images even better, including a new camera (the Near Infrared Camera and Multi-Object Spectrometer, or NICMOS) that excelled at taking infrared images and a new spectrograph (the Space Telescope Imaging Spectrograph, or STIS). At the same time, the astronauts removed two outdated instruments—the Goddard High Resolution Spectrograph and the Faint Object Spectrograph—to make room for the new ones.

The NICMOS was an especially exciting addition. Its infrared vision allowed *Hubble* to see things it couldn't see before—especially the dusty centers of galaxies, where stars and planets formed. It also gave *Hubble* a way to see more distant galaxies than it could before. These galaxies are "red-shifted." That is, their wavelengths are shifted toward the red end of the spectrum because the expansion of the universe is carrying these galaxies away from us.

The STIS is a versatile instrument that will allow scientists to take detailed pictures of objects in the universe. It will also be useful in the hunt for the mysterious phenomena known as *black holes*. No one has actually ever seen a black hole because they are so dense that no light is reflected from them. For this reason, their existence has been considered theoretical.

The *Discovery* crew spent ten days servicing *Hubble*. When engineers designed *Hubble,* they made this job easier by designing handholds and footholds on *Hubble*'s exterior. They also made each instrument modular so that a repair crew could pull any one of them out the way you can pull drawers out of a dresser. To make an exchange, crews would just pull the old one out and push the new one in.

The astronauts also mended some torn places in *Hubble*'s skin that were caused by constant collisions with micrometeoroids and orbiting fragments. They also replaced its old-fashioned reel-to-reel recorder with a new, solid-state microchip-based recorder. The new recorder stores ten times more scientific information from *Hubble*'s instruments than did the old recorder. That means that *Hubble* has much more space to store data before having to relay them to Earth.

A third servicing mission took place in December 1999. This time, it was an emergency. Two of *Hubble*'s six gyroscopes had worn out. The telescope could continue to operate, but the loss of another gyroscope could cause real problems. The telescope had placed itself into

Red Shift and the Expanding Universe

The objects astronomers study are so far away that no one will ever study them up close. Throughout centuries of watching the skies, astronomers have figured out a lot of tricks for learning about the universe from a great distance. For example, they use the spectrum of light given off by a star or reflected by a planet to find out what these objects are made of, how hot they are, the direction they are moving, and lots of other information.

Scientists can tell whether a star is moving toward our galaxy, the Milky Way, or away from it. First, they know what the spectra (plural of *spectrum*) of different types of nearby stars look like. So if a distant star of the same type gives off a redder light than expected, astronomers say the star's light is "red-shifted."

To understand what that means, let's take a look at another piece of the puzzle: the Doppler effect, named after the Austrian physicist Christian Johann Doppler (1803–53). For a long time, people had noticed that a moving object seemed to make a higher-pitched sound as the object approached. Sounds made by objects moving away seemed to drop in pitch. For example, the wail of a police siren seems lower in pitch as it moves farther away. In other words, the frequency, or pitch, gets lower as the source of the sound moves away from the listener. The wavelengths of the sound grow longer. In 1842 Doppler pointed out that the same pattern occurs with light waves—since light is just another type of wave that follows the same rules as sound. As a luminous object—such as a star or galaxy— moves away from an observer, the light it emits becomes redder, or is red-shifted. That is, the wavelengths grow longer. As the light from an approaching object comes toward the observer, it becomes bluer, or is blue-shifted. That is, the wavelengths grow shorter.

When Edwin Hubble applied this principle to viewing distant galaxies in 1929, he observed by their red shift that they were moving away from us. He reported that the universe is expanding—an observation that the *Hubble Space Telescope* has helped confirm.

---

safe mode. This meant that no scientific work could be done by the telescope until repairs were made.

A crew of astronauts had been training for a third repair mission, but it came a little earlier than planned. *Discovery* lifted off on December 19, and the crew captured *Hubble* two days later. Four mission specialists—including Claude Nicollier from the first repair team— replaced all six gyroscopes with updated models. They also did other housekeeping and installed an advanced main computer that is twenty times faster and has six times more memory than the original model.

The "house call" approach to servicing the space telescope has worked extremely well and has lengthened the life of *Hubble* at least another five years, and perhaps ten. What started out to be disappointing has become an exciting, ever-improving instrument that continues to make spectacular contributions to human understanding of the universe in which we live.

Astronauts John M. Grunsfeld and Steven L. Smith work on the *HST* in December 1999.

Chapter 5

The Outer Limits of the Universe

Telescopes are "time machines" that allow astronomers to look back in time. As you look out into the universe, your view is caught in another era, far, far back in time. You cannot see what faraway galaxies look like now. They are so far away that the light we see today started its voyage across the universe eons ago. Many of the stars you will see tonight don't even exist anymore, although the light they have given off is still traveling through space.

The deeper astronomers probe into "deep space," the farther back in time they see. Light from these faraway galaxies has had to travel for millions or billions of years to reach your eyes—or a CCD attached to a telescope. So when astronomers observe these objects, they are able to capture a snapshot of what things were like long, long ago. It is as if they were looking at a fossilized record of what the universe was like not long after it began. Most scientists think the beginning of the universe took place with an event called the big bang.

According to the big bang theory, everything in the universe as we know it was produced by a single, cataclysmic event that took place at the beginning of time. All the matter of the universe was crammed into an incredibly tiny space about 1/6 of a *light-year* (the distance light can travel in one year) in diameter that was infinitely dense. Evidence from many sources leads scientists to think an enormous explosion (the big bang) took place about ten to twenty billion years ago. This gigantic blast scattered matter in every direction, and the universe has been expanding ever since.

Large telescopes mounted on mountaintops on Earth's surface can see as far as *Hubble* can. But *Hubble*'s eye above the atmosphere has sharper vision—a view of the stars without their twinkle.

We know now that the universe is expanding, but no one knows for certain how it began or what will happen to it in the distant future. For these important cosmological questions, more exploration, study, and calculation are required. Astronomers and cosmologists are steadily becoming more sophisticated in their observing instruments and techniques. As they do, they will become more and more able to measure the quantity of matter in the universe—and how much time has passed since the universe was created.

In the meantime, the more we know about the makeup of the cosmos—its objects, their masses, their volumes, their structures, and how they are arranged—the more we will know about the

The Expanding Universe

The *Hubble Space Telescope* is named after Edwin Powell Hubble, who longed as a boy for adventures in faraway places. However, his father was a lawyer, so Hubble set out to become a lawyer as well. After receiving degrees in mathematics and astronomy at the University of Chicago in 1910, he studied law as a Rhodes scholar at the University of Oxford in England. He returned to the United States in 1913 and set up a law practice in Kentucky.

However, the decision just didn't feel right. The following year, he left his practice and returned to studying astronomy at the University of Chicago and its Yerkes Observatory in Williams Bay, Wisconsin. He completed his Ph.D. thesis in astronomy in 1917. That same year, the United States entered World War I (1914–18), and Hubble enlisted in the infantry to serve in France. He began as a private but was rapidly promoted to major.

When the war was over, Hubble picked up his astronomic research where he had left off. He accepted a position at the Mt. Wilson Observatory in southern California and spent the rest of his working life there. During that time, he studied what looked like glowing space fog, the cloudy-looking features known as nebulae. At the time, astronomers weren't sure whether all nebulae were patches of dust and fog. Some definitely were, but were some of them "island universes" consisting of stars? He used the massive 100-inch (2.5 m) reflecting Hooker telescope to peer at the Andromeda Nebula and was able to discern stars near its edge. This discovery proved that galaxies composed of stars must exist beyond our own galaxy. As a result, the object he studied, once known as the Andromeda Nebula, is now known as the Andromeda Galaxy. Hubble also developed a classification system for galaxies, which is still in use today.

structure of the universe itself. We will also begin to get answers to some of our most fundamental questions, such as: How old is the universe? How much mass exists in the universe? How many galaxies? How far away are the most distant objects? How quickly is the universe expanding?

Among the objects that astronomers believe to be most connected to these questions are galaxies, black holes, and quasars.

Edwin Hubble is best known for an astounding discovery he made in 1929: The farther away a galaxy is, the faster it is moving away from us. So galaxies twice as far away are receding twice as fast. This insight, which helped astronomers understand that the universe is expanding, is considered one of the most important insights of the twentieth century and is now called Hubble's Law.

Hubble's discovery is the foundation for the big bang theory about the origins of the universe. The big bang theory says that the universe began with an enormous explosion and has been expanding ever since.

For the rest of Hubble's life, he went on exploring the farthest reaches of the universe with a telescope. What more appropriate name could be given to the space telescope than the name of the man who was the first to show that our entire universe is made of separate galaxies that are isolated by deep space?

Edwin P. Hubble looks through the reflecting telescope at the Mt. Wilson Observatory near Pasadena, California.

Galactic Mysteries: Black Holes and Quasars

Astronomers have long been mystified—and very curious—about what goes on in the hearts of galaxies. These central areas seem ablaze with activity. Crowds of objects are concentrated there, including stars, dust, and gas, which seem to compete for room. In these same regions, astronomers also find quasars—starlike objects that emit bright blue light, have extreme red shifts, and often emit radio waves.

What is going on? More accurately—what *was* going on millions and billions of years ago, when the light we now see first began its journey through space?

Stars No One Can See

Some astronomers reasoned that something must lurk in the hearts of galaxies. They figured that there must be objects with tiny diameters—probably collapsed stars with enormous masses. This great mass would create an enormous *gravitational field*. So the collapsed star would take in matter and stuff it away in its tiny, central core of enormously dense, compacted matter.

At first, the very existence of such an object was just a theory. This theory was based on the laws of physics, and scientists knew it was possible, but no one had ever seen one. In fact, astronomers called such objects "black holes" because no one could see them.

Astronomers had to detect the existence of black holes in a different way. To find black holes, they used the same methods they use to find planets revolving around other stars. Even though extrasolar planets (planets not found in our solar system) are not easily visualized because they are obscured by the bright light of their stars, scientists know they exist. Scientists can also see their effects on other objects around them. For example, a black hole or an extrasolar planet might affect the orbit of a nearby object. From this evidence, astronomers know these objects are present—even though no one has seen them directly.

Why can't we see black holes? These extraordinarily tiny, massive objects are thought to have such enormous gravity that light—the fastest traveler in the universe—cannot escape their gravitational fields. The region surrounding a collapsed star is governed so completely by the collapsed star's mass that in order to escape the star's gravity, an object would have to travel faster than the speed of light. (But, of course, nothing travels faster than the speed of light.) This region is known as the *event horizon* and is often visualized as a spherical zone around the massive, dead star. Light is trapped by these very dense, collapsed stars, so they no longer give off light and cannot be seen. Gravity prevents *everything* from leaving, and it all becomes part of the dead star.

Black holes became a topic of great interest at the end of the twentieth century and the beginning of the twenty-first century. However, way back in the eighteenth century, in 1798, the French mathematician Pierre Laplace was the first to put forth the idea that a star could become so massive that its gravity would let nothing escape, not even light. As a result, he said, it would be invisible. Laplace didn't use the expression "black hole," but the concept was the same.

Later, in 1917, a German astrophysicist named Karl Schwarzchild calculated that if a star's mass is compressed to a certain radius, it would become enormously dense. He worked out mathematically exactly the radius that would cause the gravitational force to be so great that nothing—not even light—could escape, and a black hole would be formed. Of course, the more matter that tumbles toward the black hole, the denser the collapsed star becomes. The event horizon is located exactly at Schwarzchild's radius—the point at which the speed of light and the speed required for escape are the same. So if our Sun had enough mass to become a black hole (it doesn't), its radius would shrink down from its current size of 430,000 miles (692,018 km) to about 1.86 miles (3 km).

The black holes at the centers of galaxies are the most concentrated masses to be found anywhere. They consist of infalling stars, dust, and gas. All that matter causes the mass to become greater and greater, creating enormous gravity—the gravity of all the matter that was already present at the galactic centers. Yet, ground-based telescopes cannot detect the existence of black holes. In fact, until scientists working with data collected by *Hubble* worked on the subject, no one could collect much real evidence of their existence.

Help from Hubble

In July 2000, *Hubble* scientists released an especially intriguing image of galaxy M87 (about fifty million light-years away). The image showed a fast-moving jet of bright material pouring out of the center of the galaxy. It was not the first time scientists had detected something strange about M87. As early as 1918, astronomers had noticed "a curious, straight ray" that stretched out from M87. In the 1950s, radio observations discovered one of the brightest radio sources in the sky to be in the neighborhood of galaxy M87. Astronomers have also noticed other jets of this kind where evidence of black holes exists.

These discoveries lead scientists to believe that a supermassive black hole lies at the center of M87. This black hole has attracted a huge mass, equal to two billion times the mass of our Sun. They believe that this huge black hole powers the jet of electrons and other subatomic particles that *Hubble* observed.

Hubble has also succeeded in providing evidence that has allowed astronomers to calculate the mass of several black holes. The telescope has shown a relationship between the size of a disk of dust and the

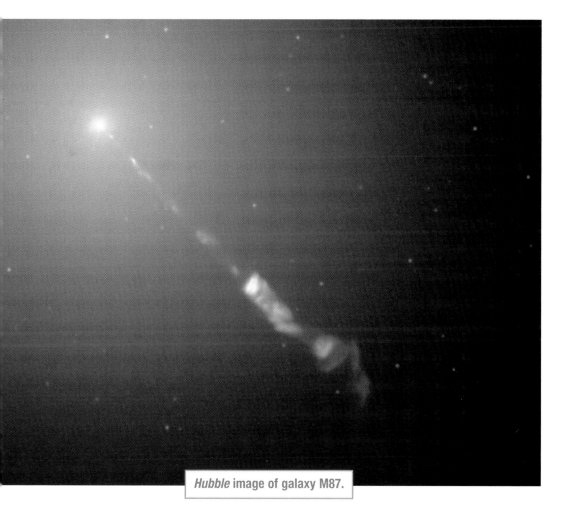

Hubble image of galaxy M87.

expected mass of a black hole at its center. *Hubble's* eagle eye and fine resolution enable scientists to calculate how fast material is spinning around suspected black holes. Black holes have inspired many speculations, and some researchers have used computer models to discover how these strange, invisible objects might work. They have also tried to figure out why different types of galaxies exist. There are many "nor-

Anne Kinney is well known as an expert in quasars, blazars (similar to quasars), and galaxies. As an instrument scientist for *Hubble*'s Faint Object Spectrograph, she had a chance to see the telescope up close before it was launched. "I was testing the Faint Object Spectrograph camera at Lockheed Martin [the engineering company that was assembling the *Hubble Space Telescope*]," she recalls. "The four-story-tall telescope loomed above me, all covered in its shiny [reflective plastic film]. Because of that experience, I have a real affection for the telescope. . . ."

Kinney began her studies of astronomy and physics at the University of Wisconsin, where she graduated with honors in 1975. She then spent several years in Copenhagen, Denmark, studying at the Niels Bohr Institute. She earned her Ph.D. in astrophysics from New York University in 1984. Since then, she has worked at the Space Telescope Science Institute in Baltimore, Maryland, where *Hubble* and its successor, the *Next-Generation Space Telescope,* both are managed.

Kinney is the author of more than seventy-five scientific papers, and she has made many public presentations about astronomy and science. Her topics of research include debris striking the inner ring of Supernova 1987A and the dynamic weather on Mars. She once provided a Mars weather report for a television station in Washington, D.C.

Kinney currently serves as origins program scientist for the *Next-Generation Space Telescope* and science program director of NASA's Origins Program. This program focuses on discovering how things began—including galaxies, stars, planets, and life.

Anne Kinney

mal" galaxies like our own, the Milky Way. However, some galaxies, known as radio galaxies or quasars, are highly luminous. Scientists think a connection may exist between the presence of supermassive black holes at the cores of some galaxies and little-understood differences among the various types of galaxies. Scientists now also think a black hole—Sagittarius A*—may exist at the center of our own galaxy, the Milky Way.

Quasar Fuel

Within the hearts of some galaxies, astronomers have also found an extremely bright type of object they call a quasar (quasistellar radio source). Quasars were discovered in the 1940s by radio telescopes. Looking like big antennae, these telescopes pick up radio waves at the low-frequency end of the electromagnetic spectrum.

Quasars offer a fascinating puzzle. They are possibly the most luminous objects in the universe. One quasar emits as much light as the entire Milky Way. In fact, Quasar 3C273 is as bright as *twenty five trillion* Suns. Yet most quasars are very small—about a hundred light-minutes across, or about the size of our solar system! They resemble stars, yet they are too big to be stars, and stars never emit radio radiation.

Quasars are intriguing in their own right, but they also offer clues to processes that took place in the universe very long ago. How? Every known quasar is extremely far away—the nearest is 800 million light-years away. These starlike objects emit unusual, bright blue lights, have an extreme red shift, and often emit radio waves. Some quasars are high-variable—their light output varies as you're watching, in a matter of minutes, in unpredictable patterns.

What could be the energy source for these brightly burning "light-bulbs"? Astronomers now suspect that the energy released when matter spirals toward massive black holes is the energy source of these beacons. That is, as gases are "swallowed" by a black hole, their gravitational

energy is converted into radiation, producing the light source for quasars. *Hubble* played an important role in these discoveries. *Hubble* confirmed that the brightest quasars do reside inside galaxies. Also, further evidence from *Hubble* showed that mergers, or collisions, between galaxies are often taking place in regions of space where quasars are found. So *Hubble* scientists realized that where they saw colliding galaxies that eject a lot of dust and gas, they also saw large quantities of matter swirling toward black holes. Both of these

In this image taken by the *Hubble Space Telescope*, a quasar is seen merging or colliding with its companion galaxy.

processes produce a lot of activity, which helps power the small, energetic objects known as quasars.

Piling It On

These pieces of evidence from *Hubble* are exciting signposts pointing down a path of exploration. As researchers continue to study images already taken and those to be taken in the future, more and more information will come together to help fill out the picture for these mysterious objects—galaxies, quasars, and black holes—and how they relate. So far, *Hubble* has provided a lot for astronomers to think about.

Taken by the *Hubble Space Telescope* in April 1995, this photo shows the gas pillars in the Eagle Nebula.

Chapter 6

Stars and Their Life Cycles

The life and death of stars has become a subject of growing interest among astronomers since the beginning of the twentieth century. These familiar objects in the nighttime skies undergo complex evolutionary processes, and the *Hubble Space Telescope* has documented many colorful details of them.

Young Stars

Images of the nebula NGC 604, an enormous cloud of gas and dust, show that stars are being born there. In this vast nursery three million light-years away, researchers estimate that more than two hundred young stars exist that are fifteen to sixty times the mass of our Sun. The nebula is illuminated by their radiation as they glow within its cloudy mass like hundreds of bright candles.

The spectacular Eagle Nebula (M16), which is about seven thousand light-years away, also harbors emerging new stars. The striking columns or stalks that reach out from this nebula show regions know as EGGs (evaporating gaseous globules) near the tips of the stalks. Astronomers suspect that these regions contain star nurseries. The fingerlike formations of the stalks are anchored in a huge cloud of cold hydrogen. The columns themselves have diameters measuring several light-years across. They are at least a light-year in length and are filled with dense, cool gases. These gases may be dense enough to collapse on themselves—the beginning stages of star formation. Infrared images of these regions show contracting, warming dust clouds. These clouds are on their way to becoming stars.

Young Stars with Young Families

Hubble has also captured visual proof that young stars commonly are surrounded by flat, pancake-shaped disks. These disks contain the raw material for the formation of planets, so astronomers expect to find planets around quite a few other stars besides our Sun. In fact, they already have found evidence of many other planetary systems. *Hubble* researchers have also noticed that jets of gas are expelled from the centers of the same disks of dust and gas in which very young stars have been found.

Like a Diamond

The new Near Infrared Camera and Multi-Object Spectrometer, installed in 1997, has captured an image of an enormously luminous star known as the Pistol Star, named after the shape of the nebula around it. This star lies about twenty-five thousand light-years away, near the center of the Milky Way. Large quantities of interstellar dust hide many of its features. However, it is ten million times more luminous than our Sun. It would take the Sun nearly four months to emit as much energy as the Pistol Star emits in one second! The dust around it is so thick, though, that no optical telescope could ever see it. The Pistol Star is visible only using the infrared camera. The infrared camera detects infrared radiation, which has wavelengths too long for the human eye to see.

If this star were an automobile, it would be a gas guzzler. Stars this massive put out so much radiation that they eat up all their fuel in a short time and burn out quickly. The end of the life of this type of star is often violent and dramatic. Astronomers think that the Pistol Star will shed its mass in a series of violent explosions in about one to three million years. The gas nebula around the Pistol Star shows that it already has seen some violence. In fact, eruptions in the outer layers of the star may have created the nebula in the first place.

Questions abound about where this massive star came from and why is it so much more luminous than other stars. It is possible that the Pistol Star is not just one star, but several. Only more study will answer these questions for astronomers.

Strange Superstar

Eta Carinae, located more than eight thousand light-years away, is a superstar surrounded by an enormous gas nebula. This superstar is four million times more luminous than the Sun and is one hundred times as massive. It is one of the most massive stars in the galaxy. Astronomers estimate that Eta Carinae will become a giant star soon— in as few as 100,000 years. This may not be soon in terms of a human lifetime, but on the astronomical scale, that's a short time period. Then

The super star Eta Carinae is more than 8,000 light-years away from Earth. This photo was taken by the *Hubble Space Telescope* in June 1996.

it will begin the final stages of its life—first becoming a supernova and finally a black hole or a neutron star.

Eta Carinae is visible only in the southern hemisphere, near the Southern Cross. Since 1677, when astronomer Edmund Halley catalogued it, it became brighter, then much brighter, faded briefly, and after that grew steadily brighter. It reached its peak brightness in April 1843, becoming the second brightest star in the sky after Sirius. It put out as much light as about five million Suns. Matter ejected from Eta Carinae during this bright period caused the star's light to appear to fade to observers on Earth. This "dust storm" has only just begun to expand to let the star's brightness show through again.

Hubble was able to obtain a clear picture of Eta Carinae, thanks to image-processing techniques. Many interesting features are visible in the matter ejected by this energetic star, including two large, polar clouds and a thin disk at the equator that streak out into space at a rate of 404 miles (650 km) per second.

Using two images of Eta Carinae, and its nebula taken at different times, scientists have shown how furiously this pair of gas and dust clouds is expanding. The star also changes its spectrum every five and a half years or so and experiences waves of increased X-ray emission every eighty-five days. The meaning of these patterns is not yet certain, but some researchers think that Eta Carinae is actually a binary system (two stars orbiting each other) with an orbit that is completed every five and a half years. If this is true, Eta Carinae is the most massive binary system ever to be discovered.

Supernova!

A supernova—or exploding star—is one of the most exciting and interesting astronomical events ever observed. Only a few have occurred in a time and place close enough for astronomers to get a really good look. The first in recorded history created the Crab Nebula in 1054, and observations were set down at the time by Chinese and Japanese astronomers. Until 1987, only two others had been

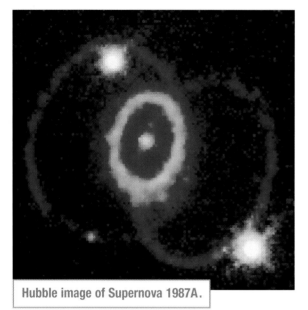

Hubble image of Supernova 1987A.

recorded—one in 1572 by the Danish astronomer Tycho Brahe (1546–1601) and the other in 1604 by German astronomer Johannes Kepler (1571–1630). So Supernova 1987A was a rare event that happened to take place just three years before *Hubble's* launch in 1990.

SN1987A was discovered on February 23, 1987, in the Large Magellanic Cloud, which is the galaxy right next door to ours. It was close enough for ground-based telescopes to see it, and when the *Hubble Space Telescope* was set to work, astronomers already knew where to look. The space telescope was able to capture pictures as a wave of material ejected from the doomed star that had collided with a ring of matter around the star. By the year 2000 the collision had begun to light up the central ring of material.

In the coming decade, astronomers will be watching SN1987A closely. They think that more material will hit the ring. When it does, even more light will shine on all the material in the region. By studying the changes in images of this object, scientists expect to be able to reconstruct a lot about the history of this exploding star—its birth, its evolution, and its death.

Chapter 7

Solar System Close-Ups

The eye that can see to the farthest reaches of the universe can also see very well close to home. Within the solar system, *Hubble*'s crisp views have brought faraway planets closer. The space-based observatory has captured views of Neptune's storms and the clouds of Uranus. It has also seen the weather on Mars and close-ups of asteroids. One of the most important views it has given us is the closest look ever at far-flung planet Pluto. Most fortunate of all, it was in the right place at the right time when a stream of *comet* fragments plowed into Jupiter.

A Good Look at Pluto

As Pluto turned on its *axis* in late June and early July 1994, the *Hubble Space Telescope* succeeded in capturing images of almost the entire

This photo of Pluto (left) and Charon was taken by the *Hubble Space Telescope* when Pluto was 4.4 billion kilometers from Earth.

surface of the planet. The collection of images produced the first surface map of the solar system's most remote planet. Planetary scientists, called *planetologists,* produced the map by using image-processing software to combine information from four separate images of Pluto's disk taken with the European Space Agency's Faint Object Camera, which was flying aboard *Hubble* at that time.

For the first time since Pluto was discovered in 1930, scientists were able to see some details on the surface of this tiny, remote planet, which has a diameter of only two-thirds of our Moon's diameter. The images showed many surprises. Pluto turns out to have more large-scale, contrasting areas of brightness than any other planet except

Earth. Several highly reflective areas turned up, and the images may show that Pluto has ice caps.

With these images collected by *Hubble,* Pluto was transformed from just a fuzzy, distant dot of light to a world with recognizable features. Scientists think that some of these features may be large basins and craters similar to the ones found on Earth's Moon. Most, though, are probably caused by the frosts that migrate across the surface, which are produced by seasonal and orbital cycles. During Pluto's nearly one hundred-year winter, even methane, carbon monoxide, and nitrogen gases freeze on its surface.

The bright areas captured by *Hubble's* images have the brilliance of fresh snow on a Colorado mountainside, but the darker areas seem more like dirty snow laying on a city street. Scientists suspect that ultraviolet radiation from distant sunlight and the effects of cosmic radiation have caused a sort of sooty residue to build up in these regions.

No ground-based telescope has ever been capable of getting a good image of Pluto because it is so small and distant (nearly fifteen thousand times farther away than our Moon). Pluto is also the only planet in the solar system that has never been visited by a spacecraft. Now *Hubble* has raised our curiosity even more with glimpses of this faraway world. Many scientists would like to see a mission to visit Pluto take place.

Front Seat at a Smashing Event

In May 1993, astronomers realized that an extraordinary event was about to take place. A comet named Shoemaker-Levy 9 was on a collision course with the giant planet Jupiter. The comet was going to smash directly into this enormous gas giant. No one had ever observed anything like this before. It was a chance in a lifetime to see what would happen.

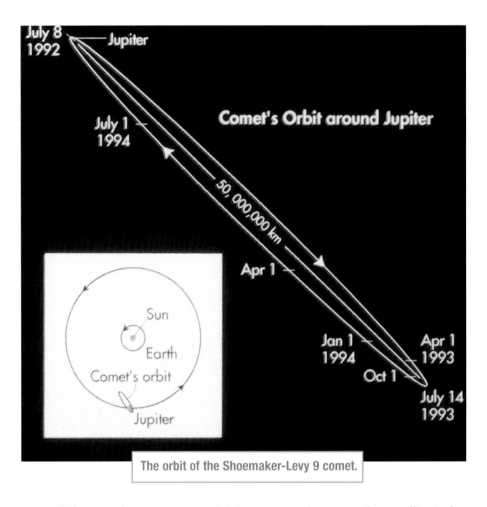

July 8
1992 — Jupiter

Comet's Orbit around Jupiter

July 1
1994

50,000,000 km

Apr 1

Jan 1   Apr 1
1994   1993
         Oct 1
              July 14
              1993

Sun

Earth

Comet's orbit

Jupiter

The orbit of the Shoemaker-Levy 9 comet.

Why was this event so rare? Most comets have very large, elliptical orbits that loop far out to the edge of the solar system and zoom in to curve around the Sun. While some do have shorter orbits, Shoemaker-Levy 9's orbit was unusual. Comet Shoemaker-Levy 9 had somehow become caught in Jupiter's gravitational field. Scientists began piecing together what had happened. Apparently, Comet Shoemaker-Levy 9 had already passed close to Jupiter several times. Each time, the giant planet had robbed some of the comet's momentum. Eventually, the comet was pulled out of its long, elliptical orbit around the Sun. It began to orbit Jupiter instead.

As scientists continued to study Comet Shoemaker-Levy 9, they learned that on July 7, 1992, the comet came so close to Jupiter that it had shattered into many fragments. Jupiter's immense gravitational field had produced tensions known as "tidal stress" in comet's *nucleus*, a ball of ice and rock. Finally the fragile comet became so wracked by the huge planet's influence that it broke apart.

Torn to Pieces

In recent years, scientists have realized that few comets or asteroids are cohesive, tightly packed objects. Usually, they have been smacked around over and over as they travel through the solar system, often disintegrating and reassembling. Some may never have fused into a single body in the first place. So they are roving "rubble piles," as Eugene and Carolyn Shoemaker once put it.

By the time Comet Shoemaker-Levy 9 was identified on photographic plates, it was bar-shaped and had several tails. Two wings of dust extended from each end of the bar. Within a few weeks, an extremely powerful ground-based telescope had captured an image of the comet. The image showed that the "bar" actually consisted of a series of nuclei that looked like a string of pearls.

Comet Shoemaker-Levy 9 had been torn into approximately twenty-one pieces. When it became obvious that this string of debris was headed straight for Jupiter, scientists began to marshal their resources to record the spectacular event from every possible angle.

Countdown to Impact

That's where the *Hubble Space Telescope* came in. On July 12, 1994, the comet was known to be nearing Jupiter's large *magnetosphere,* an area filled with electromagnetic radiation and electrically charged particles. On this date, the *Hubble Space Telescope* observed dramatic changes in the magnetosphere. For about two minutes, *Hubble* detected a large quantity of magnesium—one of the major elements present in comet dust. About eighteen minutes later, a significant change took place in the light reflected from the dust particles in Comet Shoemaker-Levy 9. From these signals scientists knew that at least one of the comet fragments had entered the cloud tops of Jupiter.

Some scientists expected the comet fragments to shatter into even smaller pieces shortly before impact. They thought the giant planet's huge tidal forces would stretch the pieces until they disintegrated.

Hubble's observations came into play again, just ten hours before impact. This time *Hubble* took a stunning image of the comet's fragments stretched out in a long row, each one distinct and solid. To most planetary scientists this was a strong piece of evidence that

July 16

July

These photos were taken by the *Hubble Space Telescope*'s Wide Field Camera 2. They show the impact of the Shoemaker-Levy 9 comet over a course of six days.

the pieces did not disintegrate. The freight train of fragments hit, one "car" at a time—moving at a speed of about 37 miles (60 km) per second. The first pieces hit on July 16, 1994, followed by four more on July 17. A few more fragments crashed into the giant planet's atmosphere each day for six days.

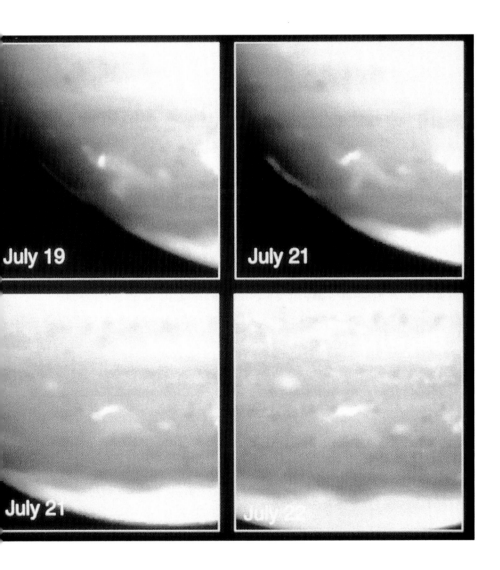

As each fragment hit Jupiter's atmosphere, it threw up a titanic fireball. Some of the fireballs had temperatures as high as about 31,940 degrees Fahrenheit (18,000 degrees Celsius). Brightness in the area increased by as much as 15 percent as each piece struck the planet.

Scientists think that the fireballs represented only a small fraction of the total energy output from the blasts. Most of that energy was probably absorbed by Jupiter's atmosphere. When comet fragments containing high proportions of ice hit the planet, they sent plumes of water spewing into space.

Within thirty minutes, huge, black clouds began to form where the fireballs had been. These dark spots looked like pancakes in Jupiter's atmosphere. Some measured up to 6,214 miles (10,000 km) across. More than one cloud was large enough to swallow up the entire Earth. The blemishes were still visible months after the collision, although the planet's constant easterly and westerly winds soon curled their edges. Eventually, the scars faded from Jupiter's complexion.

The *Hubble Space Telescope*'s Faint Object Spectrograph studied the mysterious, dark clouds and revealed a high content of sulfur-bearing compounds. Most of these compounds seemed to disperse within a few days. The ammonia that was present in the spots took several months to dissipate. The dark areas also contained silicon, magnesium, and iron—substances not found in Jupiter's atmosphere. They must have come from the comet fragments.

The impact of one fragment known as K created spectacular *aurorae* in a location that didn't usually display these light shows. Planetary scientists believe that when K hit Jupiter's atmosphere, it created an electromagnetic disturbance in the planet's magnetosphere that caused the aurorae.

Observing a Smash Hit

Comet Shoemaker-Levy 9 smashed into the night side of Jupiter—the side turned away from Earth at the time. So Earth-based astronomers had no hope of seeing the event directly. However, both professional and amateur astronomers found ways to observe its effects.

Scientists watched the edge of Jupiter's disk for signs of the impact. They observed the dark spots in the cloud tops as the planet rotated and the area that had been struck came into view. They also used instruments to measure changes in Jupiter's magnetosphere. Never before in the history of astronomy had so many telescopes and instruments been trained on one single event.

Three spacecraft, *Voyager 2, Galileo,* and *Ulysses,* also helped scientists study the collision. *Voyager 2* had finished its missions to Jupiter, Saturn, Uranus, and Neptune long before and was on its way out of the solar system. It was 3,852,500,000 miles (6,200,000,000 km) away. Nevertheless, the spacecraft used its ultraviolet spectrometer and planetary radio astronomy instrument to detect, time, and measure impact-related emissions from Jupiter.

Galileo was the only spacecraft with a direct view of the night-side areas where the comet pieces hit. Even though it was about 150 million miles (241 million km) from Jupiter, *Galileo* recorded the events as well as the best Earth-based telescopes would have done if the collision had been visible from Earth.

At the time of the collision, *Ulysses* was traveling past the southern pole of the Sun, but it could see Jupiter from there and it gathered useful information. Scientists used the spacecraft's combined radio- and plasma-wave instrument to search for radio emissions caused by the Comet Shoemaker-Levy 9 impacts.

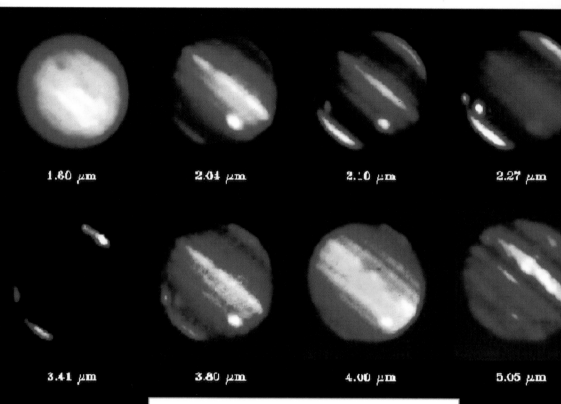

1.60 μm   2.04 μm   2.10 μm   2.27 μm

3.41 μm   3.80 μm   4.00 μm   5.05 μm

These infrared images, taken by NASA's Infrared Telescope Facility on Mauna Kea, Hawaii, show the sites of the impacts of the Shoemaker-Levy 9 comet on Jupiter.

The series of collisions was tremendously exciting, but it was also sobering. The impacts released more energy into Jupiter's atmosphere than the energy of all of Earth's nuclear arsenals combined. They had an enormous effect on the giant planet's atmosphere, and the clear message for Earth was that if it can happen on Jupiter, it can also happen here.

Two Decades of Splendor

In its first ten years of surveying the vast reaches of the heavens, the *Hubble Space Telescope* snapped 330,000 exposures, and it has focused on 14,000 targets in space. *Hubble's* gallery of data and images grows every day. It is a rich resource for today's researchers. Tomorrow's astronomers—quite possibly including you—will continue to draw upon this wealth of information far into the future.

Meanwhile, the *Next Generation Space Telescope* is gearing up for launch as early as 2007–08. The rest of NASA's constellation of Great Observatories includes three other telescopes launched between 1990 and 2010: the *Compton Gamma Ray Observatory*, the *Chandra X-ray Observatory*, and the *Space InfraRed Telescope Facility*. Using their over-lapping missions, astronomers hope to capture views of the same objects in several regions of the spectrum—including *Hubble's* and

NASA's Observatories
Vital Statistics

Telescope	Launch Date	Description
HUBBLE SPACE TELESCOPE	1990; extended in 1999	To cover visible-light astronomy, as well as near-infrared and ultraviolet portions of the spectrum
COMPTON GAMMA RAY OBSERVATORY	1991; retired in 2000	To collect data from the most violent, extremely energetic physical processes in the universe
CHANDRA X-RAY OBSERVATORY	1999	To observe such X-ray emitters as black holes, quasars, and high-temperature gases
SPACE INFRARED TELESCOPE FACILITY	2002 (planned)	To capture thermal infrared emissions blocked by the atmosphere; to orbit the Sun, trailing Earth
NEXT GENERATION SPACE TELESCOPE	2008	To pick up where *HST* leaves off

Next Generation Space Telescope's visible-light, near-infrared, and ultraviolet images; *Space InfraRed Telescope Facility*'s infrared views, and *Chandra*'s X-ray views.

Through these new images, we will begin to comprehend more and more of the wonders of the cosmos and to grasp its infinite variety, splendor, and complexity. It has been a long path from the first telescope observations made by Galileo in the seventeenth century to these sophisticated observatories in space. Today's convergence of energy, sophisticated astronomical instruments, revolutionary images, and human expertise has received an important boost from the work done by the first Great Observatory in space, the *Hubble Space Telescope*.

Vital Statistics

Subject	Before Hubble Came Along	Hubble's Views
THE RATE OF COSMIC EXPANSION AND THE AGE OF THE UNIVERSE	Scientists disagree; wide-ranging results put estimates of the age of the universe between 10 and 20 billion years old	Narrows the estimates to within 10 percent precision, indicating an age between 12 and 14 billion years
SUPER-MASSIVE BLACK HOLES	Ground-based telescopes cannot provide absolute proof of the existence of black holes	By measuring the velocity of gas surrounding a black hole precisely, *HST*s provides very strong evidence; black holes are shown to be common at the cores of galaxies
EVOLUTION OF GALAXIES	Little is known about galaxies more than several billion light-years away	Can see back to within a billion years of the big bang; *HST*'s deep imaging reveals the evolution of galaxies and the rate at which stars form

[1] Adapted from "HubbleSite: A Decade of Discovery," produced by Space Telescope Science Institute's Office of Public Outreach, http://hubble.stsci.edu/sci.d.tech/discoveries/10th/our_universe/in-depth/decade.shtml

Subject	Before Hubble Came Along	Hubble's Views
QUASARS	It's established that quasars originated early in the life of the universe; view of "fuzz" surrounding some quasars thought to be the galaxy where the quasar is located; black holes probably power quasars	*HST* clearly shows several galaxies that provide homes to quasars; some are in the process of merging with other galaxies, and these collisions evidently fuel the central black hole, which in turn powers the quasars
"STELLAR NURSERY" ENVIRONMENTS	Little is known except for detection of jetlike features and infared views of stellar disks	Disks that contain planetary material in the making surround many very young stars; disks surrounding stars direct the flow of jetlike features
USE OF REMOTE SUPERNOVAE TO INDICATE DISTANCE	Cannot distinguish the light from a supernova from the light of the galaxy in which it resides	With the help of ground-based telescopes, *HST* detects supernovae as far back as half the age of the universe; results indicate the rate of expansion of the universe is increasing
PLUTO	A brightness map of the surface is created through observation of transits and eclipses of Pluto's moon Charon	*HST* confirms the map already completed, shows a varied surface full of contrasts, and resolves Charon as a clearly separate disk

Subject	Before Hubble Came Along	Hubble's Views
SUPERNOVA 1987A	Closest supernova in 400 years is observed by a large collaboration of telescopes	*HST* is able to discern changes in the debris from the fireball and the ring of enriched gas surrounding the star
GALACTIC BULGE STRUCTURE	Views can be obtained only of the Milky Way's central bulge and those of nearby galaxies	*HST* has found out more about the formation of galactic bulges: Elliptical galaxies formed large bulges early in the universe; birth of new stars may cause small bulges due to instabilities of the galaxy's disk or collisions between galaxies

History of Telescopes: A Timeline

1608 — Hans Lippershey of the United Netherlands builds the first refracting telescope.

1609 — Italian astronomer Galileo Galilei makes the first observations of celestial objects with a telescope he built.

1663 — James Gregory is the first to think of using a mirror instead of a lens in a telescope.

1668 — Isaac Newton builds the first successful reflecting telescope.

1770s — William Herschel builds immense telescopes, as big as 40 inches (1 m) in diameter.

1844 — Lord Rosse builds an even bigger, 72-inch (1.8-m) telescope in Ireland.

1917 — The Hooker telescope, a reflector with a diameter of 100 inches (2.5 m), is completed at Mt. Wilson Observatory, Pasadena, California.

1923 — Rocket scientist Hermann Oberth publishes an article about placing a telescope in orbit.

1946 — Astronomer Lyman Spitzer writes a report exploring the idea of an orbiting telescope in detail.

1948 — The Hale telescope obtains first light at the Palomar Mountain Observatory in California. At 200 inches (5-m), it is the largest reflecting telescope in the world.

1957 — The USSR launches the first artificial satellite, *Sputnik 1.*

1972 — Launch of the first small astronomical telescope, *Copernicus,* the first of NASA's Orbiting Astronomical Observatories (OAOs).

1977 — Congress approves funding for a sophisticated space telescope, the first of NASA's Great Observatories, later named the *Hubble Space Telescope.*

1979 — NASA begins building the *Hubble.*

1990 — The *Hubble Space Telescope* is launched from the space shuttle *Discovery.*

Flaw in primary mirror is discovered; development of COSTAR (Corrective Optics Space Telescope Axial Replacement), a complex optical package to reduce distortion and slightly blurred images, is begun.

1991 — The *Compton Gamma Ray Observatory (CGRO)* is launched from the space shuttle *Atlantis.*

1992 — The Keck I 400-inch (10 m) reflecting telescope is completed at the Mauna Kea Observatory in Hawaii, atop the 13,796-foot (4,205-m) summit of Mauna Kea.

1993 — First *Hubble* servicing mission, space shuttle *Endeavour:* During EVAs, astronauts install COSTAR and perform other updates and repairs.

1996 — Keck II is completed on Mauna Kea. With its twin (Keck I), it is the largest reflecting telescope in the world and uses segmented reflecting mirrors.

1997 — Second *Hubble* servicing mission, space shuttle *Discovery:* Astronauts make five EVAs to update instruments.

1999	*Chandra X-ray Observatory,* another part of NASA's Great Observatories series, is launched and deployed from the space shuttle *Columbia.*
	Third *Hubble* servicing mission: During three EVAs, astronauts onboard space shuttle *Discovery* perform maintenance on the *Hubble Space Telescope.* The mission may extend the telescope's life for another ten years.
2000	The *Compton Gamma Ray Observatory* completes its mission and is safely brought down from orbit.
2001	Fourth *Hubble* servicing mission: Instrument upgrades to be made.
2003	(Planned) Fifth *Hubble* servicing mission: Instrument upgrades to be made.
2008	(Planned) *Next Generation Space Telescope* (*NGST* or "*Hubble 2*") to be launched.
2010	(Planned) Final servicing mission to bring *Hubble* mission to completion; plans exist to return *Hubble* to Earth so that some instruments may be reused in other telescopes.

aperture—an opening in a telescope through which light can enter

asteroid—leftover chunks of material not included in any planet during the formation of the solar system; also, part of a planet broken off by a collision

Asteroid Belt—the region between Mars and Jupiter in which most asteroids orbit

atmosphere—gases surrounding an object in space, such as a planet or moon

aurora (pl. aurorae)—displays of light caused by interaction between energetic, charged particles and a planet's magnetic field

axis—an imaginary pole or rod around which a planet or moon turns or rotates

bit—in computers, the abbreviation of *b*inary dig*it*, the smallest unit of binary data (1 or 0)

black hole—an object in space having such extreme density that it prevents all matter, as well as light, from escaping it; believed to have formed from a collapsed star (see *event horizon*)

byte—the amount of computer memory required to store one character, usually 8 or 16 bits in size

CCD—an abbreviation for "charge-coupled device," an instrument that uses a light-sensitive substance on a silicon chip to record images digitally, taking the place of a camera in many of today's telescopes

comet—a small, celestial body having a very elongated orbit around the Sun; contains a head or nucleus composed of frozen water and gases mixed with dust; when nearing the Sun, the frozen material sublimates and forms a vast cloud of gas and grit and a tail of vapor

composition—what something, such as a planet, is made of

concave—describing a lens or mirror, a shape that is thinner in the middle and thicker at the edges, giving it a scooped-out appearance

convex—describing a lens, a shape that is thicker in the middle and thinner at the edges

crater—a rimmed basin or depression in the surface of a planet or moon that is caused by the impact of a meteorite

density—how much of a substance exists in a given volume; the amount of mass in a given volume of a particular substance. Each material has a specific density—so no matter how much of it you have, it always has the same density

diameter—the distance across the center of a circle or sphere

disk—flat-looking circle we see from Earth when a planet is shining in the full reflected light of the sun

electromagnetic spectrum—the full range of the waves and frequencies of electromagnetic radiation. Radio and infrared rays, at one end of the spectrum, have very long wavelengths and are invisible to human eyes. Visible light is about in the middle. At the other end of the spectrum are types of radiation with such short wavelengths that they are invisible to humans, including ultraviolet (UV) waves, X-rays, and gamma rays

event horizon—the region around a black hole that is close enough to the central mass so that any object would have to travel faster than the speed of light to escape the gravity of the collapsed star; is often visualized as a spherical zone around the dead star

gamma ray—a type of electromagnetic radiation that has extremely short wavelengths (shorter than both ultraviolet radiation and X-rays); invisible to humans but can be recorded by *HST*

gigabyte—1 billion bytes (See *byte*)

gravitational field—the region around an object where its gravitational pull is felt

gravity—the force that pulls things toward the center of a large object in space, such as a star, planet, or moon; the attraction exerted by an object with mass. The gravity of the Moon creates the tides on Earth; Jupiter's gravity influences its moons and all nearby objects, including asteroids in the Asteroid Belt. Gravity keeps Earth orbiting the Sun and the *Hubble Space Telescope* and space shuttles orbiting Earth

gyroscope—device used to maintain orientation; for example, in a spacecraft or aircraft

infrared (IR) radiation—a type of electromagnetic radiation that has long wavelengths, just beyond visible red light in the spectrum; invisible to humans but can be recorded by *HST*

interstellar—between or among the stars

light pollution—brightening of the nighttime sky that makes Earth-bound astronomy difficult; caused by artificial lights on Earth's surface

light-year—the distance light travels through a vacuum in one year, about 5.88 trillion miles (9.46 trillion km)

magnetosphere—a vast region of electromagnetic radiation and electrically charged particles extending out from a planet; caused by the interaction of the planet's magnetic field and the solar wind

mass—the amount of material a body contains; measured in grams or kilograms. Unlike weight, which varies with gravity, the mass of an object is the same wherever it is located

meteorite—a chunk of a rock from space that has struck the surface of a planet or moon

nebula (pl. nebulae)—a cloud of interstellar gas or dust, or both

NGST—*Next-Generation Space Telescope,* the successor to the *Hubble Space Telescope*

nucleus (pl. nuclei)—the head, or main body, of a comet

optics—the optical devices (lenses and mirrors) that serve to relay light in a telescope

orbit—the path traced by an object as it revolves around another body

photovoltaic effect—the process of converting energy captured from the Sun into electricity

planetologist—a specialist in the study of planets

primary objective—the primary mirror or lens on a telescope; the first lens or mirror struck by light shining into the telescope

quasar—an abbreviation for quasistellar radio source meaning a very bright, compact, starlike object in space that is far away and is moving rapidly away from Earth

radio waves—electromagnetic signals sent out in the frequency range between about 10 kilohertz and 300,000 megahertz. Radio

waves, like all other electromagnetic radiation, travel at the speed of light, 186,282 miles (300,000 km) per second in a vacuum

reflector—a type of telescope that uses mirrors to gather light and relay images to the observer

refractor—a type of telescope that uses lenses to gather light and magnify objects

resolution—in an image or photograph, the ability to display detail. A camera having high resolution can capture extensive detail with a high level of accuracy

revolve—to move in a path, or orbit, around another object. Earth revolves around the Sun, making a complete trip in one year

rotate—to turn on an axis

solar array—a panel of solar cells, or batteries, used to convert sunlight into power

solar wind—the rush of electrically charged particles emitted by the Sun that extends far out to the edge of the solar system. in fact, the "heliopause," or edge of the solar system, is defined as the point at which the solar wind can no longer be detected

spectrograph—a device used to study the electromagnetic radiation of an object; photographs or records the object's spectrum (distribution of electromagnetic radiation)

spectrum *(pl. spectra)*—the distribution of an object's electromagnetic radiation, which can be seen when recorded in a *spectrograph* (see also *electromagnetic spectrum*)

superstar—a massive star

telescope—an instrument used to view distant objects

terabyte—1 trillion bytes (see *byte*)

tidal stress—the tension created between nearby objects by tidal force (the difference in the force of gravity exerted on the near and far sides of an object); for example, Jupiter causes considerable tidal stress on objects that pass nearby

ultraviolet (UV) rays—radiation with wavelengths just shorter than violet light; "black light" is a form of UV radiation

volt—a unit of measurement of electric potential and electromotive force

volume—the amount of space occupied by an object, expressed in three-dimensional terms, such as cubic miles, cubic kilometers, and so on

X-ray—a type of electromagnetic radiation that has very short wavelengths (shorter than ultraviolet rays and longer than gamma rays); invisible to humans but can be recorded by *HST*

To Find Out More

The news from space changes rapidly, so it's always a good idea to check the copyright date on books, CD-ROMs, and videotapes to make sure that you are getting up-to-date information. One good place to look for current information from NASA is U.S. government depository libraries. There are several in each state.

Books

Campbell, Ann Jeanette. *The New York Public Library Amazing Space: A Book of Answers for Kids.* New York: John Wiley & Sons, 1997.

Levy, David H. *Quest for Comets.* New York: Plenum Press, 1994.

Peterson, Carolyn Collins, and John C. Brandt. *Hubble Vision: Further Adventures with the Hubble Space Telescope.* Cambridge: Cambridge University Press, 1998.

Scott, Elaine, and Margaret Miller (photographer). *Adventure in Space: The Flight to Fix the Hubble.* New York: Hyperion Books for Children, 1995.

Sumners, Carolyn T., and Kerry Handron. *An Earthling's Guide to Deep Space: Explore the Galaxy Through the Eye of Hubble Space Telescope.* New York: McGraw-Hill, 1998.

Voit, Mark, and Richard Maurer. *Hubble Space Telescope: New Views of the Universe.* New York: Harry N. Abrams, 2000.

Videotapes

Hubble Telescope, Air & Space, 1997. VHS format.

Hubble Space Telescope: Rescue in Space, 1995. VHS format.

Organizations and Online Sites

These organizations and online sites are good sources of information about the *Hubble Space Telescope* and astronomy. Many of the sites listed below are NASA sites that have links to many other interesting sources of information about the solar system and astronomy. You can also sign up to receive NASA news on many subjects via e-mail.

Amazing Space
(Education Online from the *Hubble Space Telescope*)
http://amazing-space.stsci.edu
This site offers Web-based activities developed for students by the Space Telescope Science Institute. Activities cover topics from the history of telescopes to black holes and galaxies.

Hubble: Cosmic Kids
http://hubble.gsfc.nasa.gov/classrm.html
This site uses cartoon characters to explore the *Hubble* and how it works.

Hubble Site

http://hubble.stsci.edu/

A wealth of information about *Hubble* is provided on the Public Outreach site for the *Hubble Space Telescope.* It is produced by the Space Telescope Science Institute, which manages *Hubble* and the *Next-Generation Space Telescope.*

Lunar and Planetary Institute

http://www.lpi.usra.edu/lpi.html

This is the site of a NASA-funded institute that offers fascinating material about space exploration and the solar system.

NASA Ask a Space Scientist

http://image.gsfc.nasa.gov/poetry/ask/askmag.html#list

Take a look at the Interactive Page, where NASA scientists answer questions about astronomy, space, and space missions. The site also has links to archives and fact sheets.

NASA Newsroom

http://www.nasa.gov/newsinfo/newsroom.html

This site features NASA's latest press releases, status reports, and fact sheets. It includes a news archive with past reports and a search button for the NASA website. You can even sign up for e-mail versions of all NASA press releases.

The Nine Planets: A Multimedia Tour of the Solar System
http://www.seds.org/nineplanets/nineplanets/nineplanets.html
This site has excellent information about the planets. It was created and is maintained by the Students for the Exploration and Development of Space at the University of Arizona.

Real-Time Spacecraft Tracking
http://liftoff.msfc.nasa.gov/RealTime/JTrack/Spacecraft.html
Visit this site to find out where the *Hubble Space Telescope,* the *Chandra X-ray Observatory,* the space shuttle (when in flight), the *International Space Station,* and other spacecraft are located right now.

Space.com
http://www.spacekids.com
This is a site just for kids about space, astronomy, cosmology, and planetary science—with clear explanations and an easy-to-read, upbeat approach.

Welcome to the Planets
http://pds.jpl.nasa.gov/planets/
This tour of the solar system has lots of pictures and information. The site was created and is maintained by the California Institute of Technology for NASA/Jet Propulsion Laboratory.

Windows to the Universe

http://windows.ivv.nasa.gov/

This NASA site, developed by the University of Michigan, includes sections on "Our Planet," "Our Solar System," "Space Missions," and "Kids' Space." Choose from presentation levels of beginner, intermediate, or advanced.

Places to Visit

Check the Internet (*www.skypub.com* is a good place to start), your local visitor's center, or phone directory for planetariums and science museums near you. Here are a few suggestions:

National Air and Space Museum

7th and Independence Ave., S.W.
Washington, DC 20560
http://www.nasm.edu/NASMDOCS/VISIT/

This museum, located on the National Mall west of the Capitol building, has many interesting exhibits related to the history of space exploration.

Rose Center for Earth and Space

American Museum of National History
New York, NY 10024
http://www.amnh.org/rose/

Exciting displays and presentations await in this premier planetarium and space museum.

Bold numbers indicate illustrations.

Ray Spangenburg and **Kit Moser** are a husband-and-wife writing team that specializes in science and technology. They have written forty-six books and more than a hundred articles, including a five-book series on the history of science and a four-book series on the history of space exploration. As journalists, they covered NASA and related science activities for many years. They have flown on NASA's Kuiper Airborne Observatory, covered stories at the Deep Space Network in the Mojave Desert, and experienced zero gravity on experimental NASA flights out of NASA Ames Research Center. They live in Carmichael, California, with their Boston terrier F. Scott Fitz.